Help my Unbelief

Michael Paul Gallagher SJ

Help my Unbelief

Loyola University Press
Chicago

First published 1983 by Veritas Publications, 7/8
Lower Abbey Street, Dublin 1, Ireland

North American edition published 1988 by Loyola
University Press, 3441 North Ashland Avenue,
Chicago, Illinois 60657

in association with X. Diaz del Rio, S.J., Gujurat
Sahitya Prakash, Anand, India

Acknowledgments
The material in sections 10, 12, and 13 appeared in
the following journals, respectively: *Intercom, Reality,* and *Resource.* Some paragraphs in other parts
of the book have been adapted from the author's articles that first appeared in the following publications: *Concilium, Doctrine and Life, Faith Today,
The Furrow, The Irish Catechist, Milltown Studies,
The Month,* and *Studies.*

Cover design by Ellen M. Scanlon

Library of Congress Cataloging in Publication Data
Gallagher, Michael Paul.
    Help my unbelief.
    1. Faith. 2. Belief and doubt. 3. Apologetics—
20th century. 4. Christianity—20th century. I. Title.
BV4637.G35 1987   234'.2   87-17085
ISBN 0-8294-0580-1

Contents

"It were better to have no opinion of God at all, than such an opinion as is unworthy of him."

—*Francis Bacon, 1625*

*"Mere inherited faith,
in those who can have an intelligent faith
is, to say the least,
dangerous and inconsistent."*

—*Cardinal Newman*

*"To believe in You, I must believe in love and in justice;
and believing in these things is a thousand times better
than pronouncing Your name."*

—*Henri de Lubac, 1960*

Foreword

The very title of this book, **Help my Unbelief,** makes it clear that it is not meant to be a scientific disquisition on the nature of unbelief but a pastoral study of what is the problem in so many countries to-day: of loss of faith, its unnoticed erosion, its malnutrition, a distancing from it, an insensibility to it and to all ultimate questions—even in those who for some reason or other continue to pack our churches.

It is a book which reflects first hand experience. Fr. Michael Paul Gallagher, its author, is a lecturer in literature at the largest state university in Ireland and so has had over the years here (as well as in other countries through summer ministries) plenty of opportunity to listen to youth.

But it is also a book which is rooted in research. The first time I heard of Fr. Gallagher was in 1978 when I was appointed by the Holy Father to head the Vatican Secretariat for Non-Believers. In the library of the Secretariat I discovered a doctoral thesis, completed in 1980, and entitled **Approaches to Unbelief** which gave me an overview of the field in which I was now called to work in. In this research project Fr. Gallagher had investigated various developments concerning the Church's relationship with atheism and the different ways of tackling this problem adopted by centres on both sides of the Atlantic.

In the present book Fr. Gallagher has been able to communicate with the anxieties of many of the elderly about the loss of faith among young people and at the same time with the searchings of young people themselves, helping them to grow in a more personal and Christ-centred faith.

No wonder then that when the book was first published in Ireland in 1983, it was an immediate success, requiring four printings in the course of its first year. Obviously it was meeting a need in a country famed for its traditional Catholicism, a Catholicism, however, which has found itself challenged almost overnight by rapid urbanization, a growing consumerism and other socio-cultural changes.

Help my Unbelief is very relevant to other countries too where the bottom is being knocked out of an inherited faith and a conventional religion. The book has already been translated into German. Because of the success of the book with the youth in Ireland and Great Britain, friends have urged Fr. Gallagher to prepare a new edition for an international audience. This book is the result. Fr. Gallagher has removed material of specifically Irish interest and made some significant additions.

I know that Fr. Gallagher, a Jesuit, envisages his book as part of the response of the Society of Jesus to the special mandate concerning atheism which Paul VI gave it and which the present Holy Father, John Paul II, has confirmed. As president of the Vatican Secretariat which has been given a similar task I welcome the international edition of **Help my Unbelief** as an excellent contribution to the response of the Church to the challenge of modern atheism. I hope the book will bring light and courage to many of those who have distanced themselves from the Church and the Faith entrusted her by her Divine Founder and that the book may inspire more priests and religious to step out of the railings of their presbyteries and religious houses to listen to the faith difficulties of the marginalized, especially among the youth, and to walk with them in dialogue towards the God of Jesus Christ.

Easter 1987

> *Paul Cardinal Poupard*
> *President*
> *Secretariat for Non-Believers*
> *Vatican City*

Preface

This book is intended for anyone puzzled about why God seems unreal to them today. It is also intended for those troubled about people around them, perhaps very close to them, who experience this new sense of unreality in different ways: some may be disappointed with Church forms of religion; others may have lost the capacity for prayer; others still may find faith simply incredible. I think of these pages as being read by two rather different groupings of people: by young adults who seem to be "losing the faith" and who want to ponder some of the issues involved, and by a more senior group of parents, teachers, priests, or anyone concerned about what is happening in the new generation over religion.

At first when I thought of addressing two audiences at once, I feared that it would lead only to confusion. What might appeal to one group would not be heard by the other. But on reflection I began to hope that this very risk could be a strength, and so one function of this book is to attempt a dialogue between different horizons, almost a bilingual conversation, because I'm convinced that the two groups sometimes seem to be speaking two quite different languages. In recent years I have had many privileged opportunities to listen to these two languages. Through teaching for some eighteen years in University College, Dublin, I have been graced with the chance to enjoy the searchings of students through many hours of conversation. In the last few years I have been invited to communicate the fruits of this experience (and of some research I was able to undertake in pastoral theology) to many audiences of priests or teachers or parents. Both of these groups, younger and older, have been of immense help to me in shaping these chapters.

From the younger generation I learned much that I try to express in the early sections, dealing with the realities of the new faith situation.

From the older audiences I found myself forced to clarify the roots or causes of this new context, and that forms the main focus for the middle part of the book.

With both of them I found myself challenged to work out new modes of response, and these tentative reachings out will be found in the third part of this short volume. In all probability the three parts will appeal in different ways to different readers. The first part is a quick tour through the new territory for faith. It asks "what is really happening?" It tries to describe the possible crisis of faith in personal terms, without jumping to analysis or judgement.

If this first part offers a report on realities as experienced, the second part tries to provide a map through the maze of change. If we can become aware of some of the causes and patterns behind the new realities we will be less likely to be thrown by them. And so these middle sections aim at what I like to call a theology of non-panic.

The final group of chapters will try to go beyond simply understanding the situation to some ways of meeting it positively. They are intended to help the searcher towards a possible decision of faith, and they are couched largely in the form of letters to individuals or groups.

It may be worth adding a word about what this book is *not:* it is not a theodicy or set of proofs for the existence of God. It tries instead to clarify the experiences of belief and unbelief as they are shaped by today's culture. The focus is rather on the level of dispositions than of intellectual arguments—because I am convinced that the real story lies there. The key question does not concern ideas so much as fundamental attitudes. How has the openness for faith been conditioned by the new context of modern life?

Nor is this intended as a scholarly book. Footnotes have been left out. The wavelength is more middlebrow than academic, and there are several passages where I report some of my own experiences and explorations. The purpose here is quite simply to make sense, or at least to make better sense to others, through evoking the individual struggle for faith today.

It is a particular pleasure to me that a revised edition of this book will appear from India. It has been adapted to suit a more international readership. Although the roots of my experience lie within Ireland, I have had many opportunities to encounter faith situations elsewhere in the world. Ten years ago I spent a very happy half year in India. More recently I have lectured an areas of unbelief and the struggle for faith in Australia and the United States. Wherever they may be read, the author's hope is that these pages may bring hope—about faith and even more about the love that God's Spirit brings about in all of humanity.

PART ONE

Facing Realities

1

SAYING MASS AS AN ATHEIST

It was a Thursday evening at Mass that I entered into my atheism in a deeper way than ever before. That may sound like the opening sentence of a first-person novel, but in fact it is true of the author of this book. Does that seem shocking? I believe it to be a not uncommon reality, even for religious people, that they run into bouts of temporary atheism and I want to open this discussion by describing one of mine. A short experience, yes, but one that proved more revealing than other more lingering eclipses of faith.

The context may have had something to do with it—it often does. I had a short night's sleep and a longish and somewhat unsatisfactory day. The actual trigger for atheism came paradoxically with the reading of the Gospel at Mass. It was about the Sadducees disputing with Christ over resurrection from the dead, and, with a little form-criticism in my head, I found myself disbelieving that these words were ever spoken by Jesus: they were surely put into his mouth by some controversy in the early Church. How much was added? The question soon became magnified into "how much was fabricated?" From that inner standpoint I stayed unusually alert to the words of the Mass, but in a deeply doubting vein. I found myself, as it were, watching from the outside, and hearing words with a certain nostalgia for their meaning, almost as if I had been an atheist for years and was now revisiting a familiar scene of worship. In one sense I struggled with the thoughts and movements of spirit, but it remained an alarming and lonely experience to be there with my community, and yet to feel cut off from the core of why we were gathered there. For the others it was just an ordinary evening Mass, low-key and undemonstrative. For me it was hiddenly dramatic. I wondered if I would ever emerge from this state of finding it incredible. Concelebrating, I found the words of the consecration painful in a strange way, hoping that they could be true but sensing that they were not. Through the post-consecration prayers I joined in the words, wishing that the living and the dead could be blessed, but fearing that it was all a sham, a facade on human fears. The whole liturgy seemed a rich symbolic wisdom with only imaginary foundations: It was what mankind had built around the story of Jesus. Sharing the sign of peace with others was an experience of sadness; we thought we were giving one another something from God but we might have only one another, alone in the world. More intense still was the moment of holding the host prior to communion, because it was a stark either-or: true or false, with no middle ground. Either this bread was the presence of Jesus or the whole thing was fantasy. Either the Resurrection was an event, or the whole edifice of our religion was a grotesque exaggeration of one preacher's life in Palestine.

After receiving communion I found myself praying or trying to pray, using the famous words from the father of the possessed boy in the gospels: "Lord, I believe, but help my unbelief" *(Mark 9:24)*. I simply repeated them inside myself. Nothing much happened and yet something changed. Perhaps I can best express it by borrowing two utterly simple words from the end of George Herbert's sonnet on prayer when, after listing phrase after phrase for the range of the experience of prayer, he concludes that it means "something understood".

What did I understand or begin to understand after communion and at the close of my Mass in atheistic mood? I understood that faith was a more extraordinary gift than I had ever realised. I glimpsed the potential doubt that can never be separated from faith in this life. Most of all I came to see, yet again, that faith is something quite different from mere accuracy of objective truth. My bout of doubt had been born within a knowledge framework and then broadened out into a general mood of negative vision.

As I sat there after communion my thoughts were more simple than this explanation: I came up against the fact that if faith were possible at all, it would be more a matter of life and of love than of truth on its own. Only within a certain disposition or attitude can faith be found. When I moved from sceptical distance to some attempt to pray my inner stance changed. As the *Magnificat* put it: "the hungry he fills with good things, the rich he sends empty away". I was re-learning that distinction from within. By the end of Mass my outlook had expanded towards "hunger". I was still fragile, still a little frightened and unsure. But there was "something understood", and it was to clarify itself.

That evening I found myself describing this whole experience to a few others in my community. It was part of an occasional gathering we have to share something of our inner lives, and it seemed only right to take the opportunity to express my most recent struggle. This too marked an important if obvious discovery.

Was it not Dostoevsky who said that atheists are those who have lost contact with ordinary people? As I recounted my experience at Mass earlier, I found myself seeing it with a certain calm because I was hearing myself through the understanding of others. It did not lessen its reality, but it gave it a less isolated perspective. "Man is not meant to be alone", as Genesis says. Perhaps faith cannot easily stay alive without some community.

I emerged from that bout of unbelief in a sober frame of mind but strengthened. I chose to begin this book with it because it may serve to evoke the reality of other people's struggles. It may also suggest a few important ways of coping with doubt: non-surprise first of all; keeping the door open to hunger; and keeping some lines of communication with others too.

Reflecting on what I was calling "temporary atheism" may also purify one's appreciation of faith. The gospel episode that came to sum it up for me is in the eighth chapter of Mark, where we hear of the cure of a blind man. Often blindness in the gospel can be taken as both literal and symbolic of some faith-blockage. In this instance other people bring a man to Jesus; he does not seem to ask much himself. Then Jesus takes him by the hand "out of the village"; being led out of the small horizons into somewhere of potentially deeper encounter is a crucial step towards new sight. But the healing does not happen fully the first time, and in this respect this story is unique in the New Testament. When the man is asked by Jesus if he can see anything, he has the courage to say both yes and no. It would have been so easy to get excited about seeing at all, but instead he admits that he is still in a blur: "I see men but they look like trees to me, walking around". This is a marvellous moment that I can identify with frequently. It is the state that I had at the end of Mass on that Thursday evening, having emerged from blindness into some vision but still a bit of a blur. Something more was needed, and for me the instrument of that fuller freedom was the chance to talk it out with others. For the man from Beth-sa'ida there came the second touch from Jesus, which allowed him "to see everything clearly", and to stop being just "the man who was beginning to see".

These three states are real: blindness, blur, vision. And it helps greatly to know where one is, even in the flux of one day and even more in the flux of a lifetime.

Finally, there is the unusual note at the close of the episode in Mark where the man is told to go home but not to enter the village. Being restored to sight is like coming home; it can be harmed by the smallness of the village. Faith involves "being sent" to others and, also, avoiding the unhelpful wavelength, the disposition of mere curiosity.

My own little Thursday story found a larger context in that Beth-sa'ida story. One starts from blindness but the place can be wrong for freedom. One may not be healed all at once; it can have stages that require honesty and courage. And if faith is restored it will carry an in-built relationship to others, a going home, a being sent. It is unlike any other kind of knowledge, in that it is born only from hunger, from glimpsing love even in a blur, and then faith finds its fullness only in being lived. The bouts of atheism can deepen one's faith and one's gratitude for its privilege today.

2

TWO PROPHETS: DOSTOEVSKY AND THÉRÈSE

The last section, embodying a kind of personal confession, was intended to evoke the fragility of our *experience* of faith and to suggest that this is one of the realities that needs to be faced. I am not proposing that faith itself, as rooted in God, is uncertain, a matter of "perhaps yes, perhaps no". The point is rather that on the level of experience one should not be too surprised to find flux. As Bossuet put it in the seventeenth century, "there is an atheism concealed in all hearts, which is diffused in all our actions." And our situation of three centuries later only serves to make this experience of the absence of God less concealed and more frequent. God is not obvious, even to saints. And therefore I want to supplement my little incident with the much more profound experiences of two of the prophets of our modern age, a man and woman whose names are not often linked: the novelist Dostoevsky and the Carmelite, Saint Thérèse of Lisieux. They were prophets in being able to fathom the crucial spiritual struggles of their own age long before most people had become aware of them, and thus they were forerunners of the crisis of faith and of culture that surrounds us now in the late twentieth century. Both of them in quite different ways became preoccupied with atheism, even though both of them remained fervent believers. More significantly, they did not concern themselves only with atheism around them in other people; rather each of them struggled with a form of atheism within their own experience.

It is just over a century now since Fyodór Dostoevsky died, and yet, in his central insights about atheism he reads like one of our contemporaries. It was a topic that obsessed him all his life, both within his own life and in his work as a novelist. In 1868 he said that he planned to write a long novel called "Atheism", but in fact this theme stretched out over the three major works he was to complete between then and his death:. *The Devils, A Raw Youth,* and most famous of all *The Brothers Karamazov.* As he said himself it was a question that had tormented him all his life long: "is it possible for a civilised man to believe?" With all his heart he came to answer yes to that question, but he was prophetic in that his portrayals of atheism in fiction have been acknowledged by many unbelievers as the best dramatisations of their position—even though they came from the pen of a convinced Christian.

For Dostoevsky the God-question was far from a purely intellectual one, and he was one of the first to explore in depth the link between atheism and the isolation of the thinker from simple human contacts and emotions. Atheism for him was never a question of the mind alone, but rather a matter of basic choice about life. He insisted vehemently that the question of God's existence would influence everything at the centre of life and society; if there is no God, then is everything morally permissible? It is against this background of his own painful searching and finding that Dostoevsky is able, in his fiction, to do justice to the lonely agony of the unbeliever and at the same time present the case against faith with frightening force. The supreme example of this is Ivan in *The Brothers Karamazov,* who embodies what is arguably the most powerful rejection of religion anywhere in literature. He offers two major reasons for his refusal of the world made by God and for his wishing to return his ticket of his experience: first, what mankind has done in cruelty to others, and second, through the famous fable of the Grand Inquisitor, what human history has done to Christ through organised religion.

> Man has invented God. And what is so extraordinary, and wonderful, is not that God actually exists, but that such an idea—the notion of the necessity of God—should come into the mind of such a wild and cruel animal as man... I don't accept harmony. I refuse it because of the love I have for humanity. I prefer to stay with my sufferings unavenged, and my anger untamed, even if I were mistaken.

Later, speaking to the Christ figure whom he has imprisoned in sixteenth-century Seville, the Inquisitor explains why the Jesus plan for human freedom was an unrealistic dream, and why that vision had to be turned into a system that worked in the world:

> What people are looking for is not so much God as miracles...

It is not the deep options of the heart that matter, nor even love, but the mystery that people must submit to blindly, even against their own conscience. This is what we have managed to offer. We have corrected your achievement, and have grounded it on miracle, mystery, and authority...People are sure that we are right, because they recall with anguish the burden and confusion that your freedom imposed on them...We provide them with peace of mind, and quiet happiness, the happiness of weak creatures.

The sheer eloquence of Ivan's case for non-belief seems unsurpassed anywhere in the long history of atheistic philosophy, and it is striking that it should occur in a novel intended by its Christian author to be a theodicy or defence of faith. Only on one point does Dostoevsky continually portray his atheist figures as lacking: they are intellectual giants who are deeply divided within themselves and often incapable of simple love.

At the very end of his life Dostoevsky wrote in a letter about his own journey of faith: "my *hosanna* has come through the great crucible of doubt." In others words he felt personally burdened with the huge complexity of the new culture then emerging in Europe and in Russia, and he experienced within himself the divided consciousness that could easily give birth to atheism. He saw this as involving a split between attitudes of submission and of rebellion, between a brotherhood of hearts and an isolation of mere mind or mere will. From the basis of his own conflicts he was able to capture the central tensions of his whole time. In this he was both alike to, and quite different from, the woman born in France some fifty years later than himself. Both were prophets, of immense spiritual stature, and both strangely concerned with atheism. Where Dostoevsky was trained by education and social milieu to be acutely conscious of the intellectual currents of his age, Thérèse was almost entirely ignorant of the world of ideas. But both of them penetrated beneath the merely intellectual struggles to the spiritual drama of faith and atheism. And more importantly, both of these Christians entered with an extraordinary level of sympathy, into the inner world of atheism as experienced. For as will be seen Thérèse in her very different way could well echo Dostoevsky's claim to have earned her *hosanna* by enduring her version of the crucible of doubt.

The inner journey of Thérèse of Lisieux can be told largely in her own words, from her autobiography and her letters. It is there that an extraordinary story unfolds, how a young nun, who was to die at the age of 24, willingly entered into an experience of atheism.

This last phase of her life began in the early hours of Good Friday 1896 when she vomited blood, the first serious indication of the tuberculosis that was to kill her some eighteen months later. Her first response to this haemorrhage was one of welcome for the "first summons" of death and therefore of heaven, and her autobiography goes out of its way to stress the consolation and feeling that she experienced on that Good Friday:

> I had a faith so living and so lucid that the thought of heaven was the sum of all my happiness. I couldn't believe that there really were godless people who had no faith at all.

But all this freedom of spirit was to change drastically, and she was to begin a strange and painful companionship with atheists, which lasted until just before her death. In the days after Easter she tells us that "Jesus taught me to realise" the existence of "souls which have no faith". From this moment of insight into the reality of atheism, her inner life was overrun "by an impenetrable darkness", and the idea of heaven, which had previously been such a source of joy for her, became "a subject of nothing but conflict and torment". She entered a state of emptiness where "everything has disappeared", and where any effort to seek out some consolation seemed doomed to even deeper desolation. She recounts that when she tried to think of heaven she would experience only a darkness filled with the mocking voices of atheism:

> It's all a dream this talk of a heavenly country... and of a God who made it all...All right, all right, go on longing for death. But death will only give you—not what you hope—but a still darker night, the night of nothingness.

It seems incredible that this young nun, who had led the most sheltered existence possible, should now be sharing the experience of Dostoevsky and even of Nietzsche, and should be a forerunner of the drama of atheism to be voiced in similar words by so many thinkers of later generations. Yet here in 1896 we have her expressing her haunting fears that God might be mere illusion, that her hope for heaven was only a deceptive fairy-tale, and that despair was the ultimate truth.

It was these feelings of atheism that dominated the saint's inner life for the final phase of her existence. And it involved more than feelings:

> If you only knew what horrible thoughts crowd in upon me all the time! My mind is gripped by the arguments of the worst materialists.

Thérèse Martin probably did not know the name of a single major materialist, much less their philosophical positions. But at a much deeper level than intellectual debate, she took on herself the burden of modern atheism as experienced, and this became now the heart of her contemplative vocation. The whole content of faith became unreal to her, and in such a powerful way that she said she understood something of the urge to suicide. But the clearest statement of her loss of any feeling of faith also reveals the motive why she had opted for such an unexpected inner journey:

> I no longer believe in eternal life; it seems to me there is nothing beyond this mortal life. Everything is brought to an end. Love alone remains.

This was the strange secret of Thérèse, that she retained the core of faith which is love, even while suffering the loss of all emotional and intellectual sense of faith. And the love she means is two-fold: love of God and love of her "unbelieving brothers" for whom she offers her suffering of the abyss. In spite of the blitz of her emotions and thoughts, she never swerved in her fidelity to the God she believed in:

> Although I have no feeling of faith, I still try to carry out the works of faith...I do try to live the faith, even when I get no satisfaction out of it.

Indeed she seems at times to have relished "each challenge from the enemy" and to imagine God as wanting "to know how far I will push my confidence".

Against a background of rapidly declining health, Thérèse went through her last year and a half with total spiritual dryness and constant temptations against faith. Through this experience of atheism, at least on the level of mind and feelings, she envisaged herself as called to eat at the table of unbelievers. It meant a sharing of bitterness and an entry into nothingness. Only a certain dark hope and love supported her in this spiritual agony. Even as her own faith seemed meaningless she offered her experience so "that those not yet illumined by the torch of faith may behold it at last".

How is one to make sense of this unique story? It would be easy to dismiss it as neurotic, and there is evidence that Thérèse was prone to emotional disturbance. What is less easy to dismiss is the love shining through the experience of darkness. Thérèse seems to embody the paradoxes of Psalm 115: "I trusted even when I said 'I am utterly in darkness' and when I said in my panic, 'No one can be trusted'." There are two levels here in the psalm and two levels in Thérèse. Her story seems to suggest that there are many layers in what we call faith (and many levels in what full atheism would mean too). One level includes my inner or felt experience, understanding of what is happening, the words in which I seek to interpret my experience. But there is another layer, deeper or higher than experience and interpretation of experience, it is the layer of commitment and of relationship to God. Although Thérèse suffered a total eclipse of her sense of God on the level of experience, and of her ability to find God credible on the level of understanding, she never lost her faith on the deeper levels of conviction and relationships. Through all her desolations of mind and heart she shared the agony of atheism. But her rootedness in love kept her open to God in ways she could not perceive.

Reflecting on her inner story, one discovers a nugget of hidden treasure for all who struggle over faith, and it can be stated quite simply: love is more important than explicit faith; indeed love can be the shape faith takes when darkness comes and when understanding seems impossible. To express it so baldly is to do an injustice to the power of the story of Thérèse. Hers was a prophetic vocation, even a providential one. At the very close of the nineteenth century this young woman entered a frightening inner world of atheism as experienced, and she crowned her sainthood through the ordeal. Her story, with its intensity, foreshadowed the minor agonies of many ordinary people in the century then about to begin, and now drawing to a close. But her story can also be read as a parable pointing to the purifying of faith by atheism. And as will be seen later, this purifying may be true both personally and collectively for many people in our century.

3

THE BREAKTHROUGH AT VATICAN II

In 1964, within a year of his election, Pope Paul VI singled out atheism as "the most serious problem of our time", and later that same year his emphasis found echo in the debates within the Vatican Council. One French bishop drew attention to the fact that "for the first time in the history of the Church a council is meeting in an age of atheism". The story of how the Council debates treated this topic is an exciting one in itself, and marks the birth of a new ecumenism. It inaugurates a whole new wavelength of understanding towards atheism, and calls for new levels of mutual dialogue between believers and unbelievers. One has the impression that many members of the Church have yet to catch up with official teaching in this respect. But the headline set by the Council was not arrived at without pain, nor will it be reached by individual Catholics without some similar conversion experience.

When the Council opened in 1961, there was practically no mention of atheism in any of the documents prepared for discussion. As with most issues to be dealt with, the bishops found themselves presented with statements that represented the more entrenched curial thinking—that favoured by Vatican officials—rather than the more open thinking advocated by many theologians from around the world. Part of the story of the Council is the extraordinary degree to which, on topic after topic, this vast gathering of bishops rejected the narrower mentality and gave approval to approaches that in some cases had been frowned upon in previous decades.

In the case of atheism, the Council evolved from a position of mere condemnation to one of pastoral sympathy. At first the issue was thought of in what might be called "cold war" terms of opposition to communism and to materialism. But gradually more and more bishops, from all parts of the world, began to share their own concerns about the less political and less intellectual aspects of loss of faith. The whole question began to be approached from a less defective position: the typical mentality of the fifties (and I remember with pleasure the religious lessons dominated by Sheehan's Apologetics) had been one of preservation of the faith through proofs for the existence of God. But this method was now found to be not so much untrue as inadequate to the new situation. The problem of God was not just one of truth or error, that could be solved by correct argumentation. It was more a question of how people experienced their lives in today's world and how they found meaning for their existence in the middle of a whole host of new pressures. In short, the Council debates discovered that they had to face, not simply a philosophical crisis of faith, but a much more profound crisis of culture. A different starting point was needed to understand the panorama of unbelief today.

That new starting point was mankind itself. A certain Archbishop Wojtyla proposed that the Council needed to abandon churchy language and adopt a different wavelength of exploration with modern man: it was less a matter of giving doctrine from on high, which would only mean talking to oneself, but of genuine dialogue with the world. The future Pope was voicing his strong sense of Christian humanism, approaching the mystery of God through the mystery of man. And this was the line that the Council chose for *Gaudium et Spes,* its long treatment of the contemporary world. The paragraphs that embody the new reaching out to atheism are included in the first part of this document, and so they belong within a section dealing with the "calling of the human person". If man is called to relationship with God, then an atheist can be viewed as someone who, either by conviction or by being the victim of his cultural environment, remains unaware of that relationship. Immediately it is clear that this emphasis on relationship creates an entirely fresh angle on the problem of unbelief. No longer is it simply a matter of arguments, proofs, or of militant ideologies; instead the discussion is situated on the level of what is deepest and most intimate in humanity—how one perceives the significance of life itself.

But the three paragraphs devoted to the subject of atheism were not arrived at without much debate, some of it involved a lot of disagreement. One set of speakers wanted the topic to be treated in what might be called the familiar framework of rational discourse, highlighting the faulty reasoning that would deny the existence of God. These same bishops also advocated a renewed condemnation of marxism and communism as embodying political versions of atheism. Another whole school of thought took a different line: they tended to downplay the intellectual aspects of atheism and to view it in more pastoral terms, as an experience of people in today's world. Moreover, this school wanted the Church to confess its own faults and mediocrities as giving rise to much modern rejection of God and of religion. To quote from a speech of Cardinal Seper of Yugoslavia:

> A partial responsibility for this modern atheism rests with those Christians who used to defend, or who still defend, obstinately and in the name of God, the established order and the unchanging set of social structures.

Over a period of some two years the Council opted for an exciting new Catholic attitude towards atheism. At the root of this evolution lay a new awareness of the realities of the modern situation. Bishops listened to their colleagues from very different backgrounds and gradually it came home to them that one could no longer treat this question of unbelief in the old categories of proofs and politics. One could no longer speak of atheism in the singular, as if it were some unified and easily defined phenomenon.

The debates in Rome heard of many different forms of atheism from around the globe, ranging from the crisis of religious practice in French Canada to the practical atheism or religious indifference of Europe, or from the denial of God through injustice in the Third World to the more systematic and government-backed atheism of the so-called Second World. Once again the text of *Gaudium et Spes* was to mirror this variety, and the final document lists some fourteen different types of unbelief. To simplify these, one might see them as falling into four families.

First, there are the more intellectual forms of denial of God, whether stemming from a scientific mentality that claims a monopoly of truth for its own methods, or from more agnostic attitudes which hold that the question of God can never be answered.

Second, there are more humanist stances, which put so much emphasis on man's freedom as to make God seem an intruder or an enemy to human dignity; under this general heading the Council included the marxist type of atheism (without directly naming it), thus giving it much less prominence than in pre-conciliar Catholic approaches.

Third, there are what one might call false gods and false images of God; so often what is rejected as God turns out to be a distortion of the revelation of God in the gospels.

Fourth, there is a whole group of unbelievers who are more the passive victims, or products of social change, than people who consciously choose to reject God or religion.

What has been summarised in these last paragraphs will be found to be a paraphrase of Section 19 of *Gaudium et Spes*. However, it is worth standing back from the text itself to reflect both on its historical importance, and on its continuing relevance to us nearly a quarter of a century later. It was only with a good deal of searching and listening that the Council found itself forced to confront this reality of our modern world, and above all, to see this reality with new eyes. It is therefore an extraordinary moment, when for the first time in the Church history a Council takes atheism not only seriously but sympathetically. The old anathemas gave way to an honest attempt to describe the realities of unbelief in our contemporary world, and to enter into the hidden causes troubling the minds of atheists, instead of launching crusades against them. Indeed it was now possible to speak with unprecedented respect of atheists as often "endowed with breadth of mind, impatient with the mediocrity and self-seeking contaminating society today" (The words are from Pope Paul's encyclical *Ecclesiam Suam*, mentioned at the beginning of this section).

Vatican II, therefore, marked a breakthrough in official Church attitudes in its opening up to the realities of unbelief today. This realism is seen in three principal achievements of the Council:

(i)   a new sense of the complexity of unbelief;
(ii)   a new level of sympathetic understanding of unbelievers;
(iii) a desire for mutual dialogue between believers and atheists.

Just thirteen years before he was elected Pope, Archbishop Wojtyla was in fact the final speaker in the debate on atheism at the Council, and his contribution then has become of special interest since. A few sentences from it can now embody the new stance adopted by the Council:

> It will help to approach the problem of atheism not just as a denial of God, but as an inner state of the human person. Of course that situation can be studied with the methods of sociology and psychology, but a full understanding of it is possible only in the light of faith.... With this light, atheism is a problem of the human person in his inner life, a problem of the spirit, of mind and of heart.

★　★　★　★

Before closing this section on the significance of Vatican II, there remains another important development of relevance to unbelief. The Council took a particularly open and fresh stand over the question of the salvation of unbelievers. One recalls today, with some embarrassment, the story of St Francis Xavier telling the Japanese in the sixteenth century that their ancestors were all in hell. And their response was to want to be wherever their forefathers were! This extreme version of an older theology of baptism and of faith had its more moderate successors even into this century. Without being quite the official teaching of the Catholic Church, it was a common assumption that a person could not remain an atheist throughout an entire lifetime without at least endangering his or her ultimate salvation. Even now this much-debated issue can come painfully alive for parents who see their offspring abandoning church-going, or faith itself, and perhaps deciding not to have their children baptised. For people worried about their loved ones in this regard, the new optimism of Vatican II can come as a real consolation.

On three occasions the texts of the Council touch on this question, and when all three are taken together they add up to a major clarification in official teaching. The three places are *Lumen Gentium* 16, *Gaudium et Spes* 22, and *Ad Gentes* 7. What emerges is that it is not essential to have arrived at an 'explicit knowledge of God' in order to belong within the possibility of salvation. This possibility 'in some way known to God' is available to everyone, even to unbelievers. Personally I have seen many anxieties lessen when awareness of this official Church teaching sinks in. It does not diminish my hope to share with others the blessings of explicit faith, but it looks on the ultimate destiny of those who seem to reject God with a deeper and double reverence—a reverence for God's hidden ways in each heart and life, and a reverence for the conscience and the freedom of each person. In this as in so many other ways the Council set a new tone for the understanding of the deeper realities of faith in today's complex world.

4

SIGNS OF THE TIMES: IMPRESSIONS AND STATISTICS

A few years ago I spent some weeks during the summer in an inner city in the north of England. I was attached to a Catholic parish, taking over from the usual priest and allowing him a well deserved break. Apart from some essentials such as morning Mass it was entirely up to me how I would spend my time. I soon discovered that if I stayed within the railings that surrounded the church, the presbytery and the parish club, I would be kept moderately busy. There would be the occasional caller to the door, often to get some certificate or signature. There would be chat with the regulars around the club. And there would always be odds and ends of business within the house. But there I was in the middle of a riot situation, because I happened to arrive into an area that erupted on a few occasions that summer; and yet I could stay literally shielded behind the strong railings and remain out of touch with what was going on in that district.

I could personally remain untouched by the realities and it took a conscious decision on my part to counter that danger. I made up my mind that I would leave the enclosure every morning at ten o'clock, and that I would certainly not return before lunch-time at the earliest.

The first day or so outside, wandering round a tense neighbourhood, whether on foot or bicycle, proved unevenful and even empty. One morning I remember helping a man lift a lawnmower out across a locked garden gate, and wondered afterwards if I had been an accomplice in a theft. It was that kind of area. But gradually my encounters began to deepen, and indeed became mutually fruitful. I learned enormously from some of the unusual people I now had time to listen to: from exprisoners to exprostitutes (and some without the "ex"), from pickpockets to murderers, from black militants to policemen.

I spent several hours one day in the employment exchange,

sometimes in lengthy conversation, sometimes just soaking in this unfamiliar world. And that is my point here: how easy it is for church people to ignore realities that we know exist, but which we have never encountered face to face.

Applying my lived parable to the unbelief theme, it is very easy to stay behind the church railings, literally or metaphorically, and so evade one of the signs of the times, the many faces of atheism today.

Partly by the providence of my own life, which has meant that well over half my years so far have been spent in universities, either studying or teaching, I have been forced to venture beyond conventional church contacts. The accumulating experience of those years has forced me to become aware, in ways not open to some of my fellow priests, of the crisis of credibility that many young people now run into over religion and church.

One thing seems absolutely clear to me: for the majority of young people I have known the main problem of faith has to do more directly with Church than with God. But then the Catholic Church has had a "high profile" in Ireland, and church practice has been dominant and central in what their parents understand of religion. At first sight it might seem that the Irish experience is unrepresentative and unlikely to cast light on the very different situations found in larger and longer industralised nations. But on reflection this contrast is not as clearcut as might appear. Of course the religious scene in Ireland is shaped by the fact that it has emerged from a largely rural culture only since the sixties. Until then Ireland remained a highly traditional society, protected in many ways from the outside world; it had, for instance, stayed neutral during the war of 1939 to 1945. As will be outlined further in chapter six here, dramatic levels of social and economic change began in the late fifties, and during the sixties Ireland shared with other countries the new and world-wide phenomenon called 'youth culture'. This book was originally written to clarify what seemed to be happening in the young adult world influenced by all those changes. Part of its argument was that from the point of view of arriving at maturity of Christian faith, there is increasingly little difference between growing up in Dublin or Detroit, in Manchester or Melbourne. What I first heard from my contacts with Irish university students has been verified in other accents elsewhere. Of course there may be considerable differences of context but there is now a strangely predictable uniformity of youth when faced with institutional forms of religion. And so what I discerned in Ireland seems true of many other places as well.

What I have found is that the bottom has fallen out of conventional religion for many of those under thirty. What their parents believed and practised sincerely as "the faith" has turned them off. What they were taught as religion in schools has gradually bored and even embittered them. What they experience for the most part in church on Sunday is a dull ritual that does not express anything meaningful for them. The result is that their image of church, and of faith, is not something worth growing into. So they "lose the faith", or perhaps more accurately, they lose hope that what is seen as "the faith" could ever again come alive in their lives.

Let me illustrate this with two pieces of writing, one from a novel and the other from a young person on a retreat expressing his disaffection with religion as experienced. In the early seventies John Broderick published *An Apology for Roses,* a story which explores the attitudes of the emerging middle class in a small town. In the closing pages of the book the young couple are planning their wedding. Although religion seems irrelevant to them, they have to go through the formula of a church marriage to please the family. Are they going to receive Communion? That would mean going to Confession, which would make each of them feel "an awful hypocrite". So they decide to say nothing in advance of the ceremony, but simply not go to Communion. And this conversation ends ironically with Marie warning Brian that he will have to conform by starting to go to Mass again after marriage:

> It isn't so bad once you get into the habit, which is all it is really. I don't think there's any point in making an issue of it. After all, neither of us care that much anymore. I wonder if anyone really does. And you meet people, keep up with the news and that sort of thing. Although of course the sermons are diabolical.

This fictional situation can easily be mirrored in actuality. There seem to be many young couples hanging on to church practice for various superficial reasons, but with decreasing depth and commitment. This tone of cynical non-belonging can accompany a minimal conformism.

A quieter and less disillusioned sense of confusion over Church is voiced in the following statement, written by David, a bank official in his mid-twenties:

> Yes, I continue to go to Mass pretty regularly—but why I don't know. It's not simply to please the parents because I often go even when away from home. It's out of some sense of God but, like my hair, that sense of God is receding slowly. I hardly ever go to communion, and I seldom feel in touch with God through Mass. My impression is that most of my friends, even if they practise, are completely untouched by it. It's something vaguely "good" or safe that we keep doing because it seems better to go than not to go. Faith isn't dead for me but it's not too alive either, and I suppose I come away most Sundays a bit disappointed, as if I was looking for something that I never get. There are times when I doubt the whole thing, but for some reason I still hang in there.

From a priest's point of view, it is sobering to reflect that in one's congregation on a Sunday morning, as well as the majority of settled believers, Marie and Brian are sitting there, and so is David. In an article in *Doctrine and Life,* October 1982, the sociologist of religion, Máire Nic Ghiolla Phádraig has analysed the possible permutations of believers and unbelievers, using three major components of religious expression: practice, beliefs, values. Out of these she constructs a fascinating diagram of pluses and minuses showing eight possibilities in all.

Ideally one hopes that those who bother to come to church on Sunday will be believers and committed to Christian values in their way of life. David would surely merit a plus on all three, and yet he is not receiving the nourishment he seeks; in fact he is accusing the Church of not challenging him to a full life of Christian values in action. One would classify Marie and Brian quite differently: probably a plus for mere external practice and a minus on both other counts.

Almost willy-nilly, one often finds any discussion of Catholicism and young people being sucked into the narrow question of Mass attendance. In one way it is understandable in that the Church has tended to put an extraordinary amount of emphasis on this area of practice, so much so that it comes across to young people as a paradox: on the one hand they get the message (wrongly) that being a Catholic is defined by this one area of Mass attendance, and on the other hand what they experience in church on Sunday is often an impoverished level of celebration of the Eucharist. It often appears to them as a boring and individualistic duty with little or no impact on life. They frequently complain that it is performed as an unprayerful ritual, with neither depth nor much attempt to create a human community among those present.

These impressions would seem to be supported by Liam Ryan's survey of Irish religious surveys (*The Furrow,* January 1983). What emerges there is a picture of high practice having little influence on values, of a solid institutional church fostering little on the level of spiritual experience, and of a younger generation suffering more from confusion over faith than from any definite rebellion against religion. This portrait could be summed up as one of worrying inconsistency, in that high church-going, shaky beliefs, and unchristian life-values can co-exist in many individuals. So, although there is a pastoral problem of increasing non-practice, there is also a larger problem of the non-praxis of the practising.

The huge fidelity to Mass-going is undoubtedly the greatest strength of the Irish Church; but this strength could rapidly become the greatest weakness if it fails to become more than an inherited pattern of behaviour. To adapt Marx, the opium of the clergy is a full church: it could act as a drug of forgetfulness both about the new needs of those who come to church and about the more difficult needs of those who do not come any more. In short, complacency about huge levels of practice could leave the churches a lot emptier within the next generation.

Were this outline of the realities to stop here it would be badly unbalanced. It is true that the most obvious form of "unbelief" among younger Catholics shows itself in a disenchantment with the externals of church belonging and practice on the part of significant minorities of the younger generation. Although David may be representative of many of his contemporaries, other voices need to be heard before one can round off this survey of realities.

To begin with, let me cite a very different statement of unbelief from Pauline, a young woman influenced by feminist thinking, but who also embodies a tone of more vehement rejection of religion than has been heard here so far:

I've no time for anything to do with religion any more. And don't tell me I'm just angry with the Church and perhaps I deep-down believe in God still. I hate the God I was given, partly because he made me so silly for so long. I used to be very frightened of sin and all that, until I was about sixteen. Even went to prayer meetings every week at that stage. But I don't want to sound bitter, because really I feel calm about it all now. I'm fully convinced that I've become a better human being since I let go of the crutch of God. I just feel sorry for so many people cramping their lives because they're afraid of that repressive God—and women in particular—who always get a poor hearing from the clergy.

Such articulate anger represents a tendency among alert and educated people to define their religious position in reaction to some unacceptable face of established religion. Some may experience a reaction in the moral area, having experienced their Catholic unbringing as painfully negative, a view brilliantly captured in the opening of one of Brian Moore's early stories: "In the beginning was the word, and the word was NO!" This "moral unbeliever" can express hostility over the hurts he received, or else he may live with a certain dull disappointment, having found God to be an impossible moral tyrant, so that it seems better to ignore him and his commands.

Others react against what comes across to them as a narrowly other-worldly obsession in religion, something that becomes a dangerous distraction from social realities today; so they reject God as an escapist fantasy, an underminer of urgency and commitment.

By way of conclusion it may help broaden the picture somewhat, and at the same time to see the types already mentioned as falling into a number of distinct families of unbelief. Most of our examples are characterised by being in reaction to a dominant religion, and this reaction could be said to divide into three major kinds: with David it was a question of dissatisfaction or vague *alienation* from the externals of church life which left him untouched; with Pauline it was more a question of *anger* and hostility to the whole world of church and faith; with Marie and Brian it was a deeper level of *apathy,* or disinterest in the spiritual horizon in any form as will be seen in the next chapter, the thesis of the three A's cover the typical psychological patterns of unbelief; the reactions may have been always there, but within the last twenty years they have shown themselves more openly, more numerously, and with more likelihood of remaining permanent.

PART TWO

Discerning the Roots

*In May 1982, at the annual meeting of the national
conference of priests of Ireland, one of the delegates came
up with a metaphor for the present pastoral situation.
The Church was likened to a ship letting in water below
the surface; the captain and crew know that there are
leaks but they prefer not to examine them too closely—
after all the old ship is afloat and moving. Another
version of this was to imagine the Church as an old car,
coughing a lot but chugging along; the driver avoids
bringing it to a garage for a check-up for fears something
even worse would be diagnosed. Or again, it may be
compared to a man hearing noises downstairs during the
night; if he lies too long in bed merely wondering what
could have fallen, the burglar may have come and gone by
the time he decides to go downstairs. What these three
priestly parables have in common is the recognition that
non-recognition of the new faith situation is a real
danger. And so it seems wise to take a different angle on
the realities that were the focus of the previous chapters
here; so far we have been evoking or describing what is
happening, but now it is also necessary to explain why
this new context for faith has developed. If we are in
search of a theology of non-panic, then it will help to
have a clear grasp of the roots and causes of the present
influences on religion. And so the various chapters within
this part of the book will be a bit more analytical than
previously.*

5

PATTERNS OF INDIVIDUAL UNBELIEF

What may be happening when an individual is moving towards unbelief or loss of faith? Are we to equate non-practice with unbelief? Would that not imply that we identify church-going with faith itself, or at least that we think of it as so essential an expression of faith that its abandonment would mean "losing the faith?" Research carried out in French-speaking Canada can help us to answer this kind of question. Until the late fifties, the province of Quebec had a dominantly Catholic and highly church-going culture, which then suddenly underwent what they have come to call "a quiet revolution". Within a relatively short space of time many changes in values happened, and one outcome was that regular Sunday Mass-going fell from about sixty-five per cent to about thirty per cent during the sixties alone. Against the background of this crisis a special pastoral centre was established in Montreal, called *Service Incroyance et Foi,* and the personnel working there took the imaginative step of spending all their early years listening to the deeper realities of their new situation before daring to suggest how best to respond to it.

Out of this phase of sensitive listening emerged some clarifications as to the typical processes which bring a person from seemingly strong church affiliation into "distanciation", as they called it, where one or other side of religion becomes dulled and one feels oneself distanced from what previously made sense.

What aspect of faith is becoming eclipsed? This is a key question to ask about any individual, or even group situation. One person may be disenchanted with sacraments, for example, but not without some life of prayer. Another may be distant from any real awareness of Christ, but not without some religious searching. André Charron, one of the staff of the Montreal centre, has outlined a pattern of progressive "distanciation", showing how a person may move from external non-practice through various stages of deeper withdrawal from the world of religion, until they finally can reach a

state of complete unbelief and even of indifference to any religious
horizons. He has listed the eight stages as follows:

1. Abandonment of regular attendance at Mass and
   sacraments.
2. Alienation from the institutional Church; this can be
   either passive or active, depending on whether a person
   has definite objection to the Church or is simply drifting
   with the secularised society.
3. Non-belonging with the Church as a community of
   believers; again some will be more passive and merely
   nominal Catholics, whereas others will cut off their links
   more consciously, even angrily.
4. Fading of Christian values in practice, where there is no
   real impact of belief on social commitment or individual
   morality.
5. Collapse of the credibility of Christian meaning for
   life—often rooted in difficulty with, or rejection of, some
   specific content of the faith.
6. Withdrawal from belonging in faith to Jesus Christ—this
   being the point in the process of "distanciation" where
   one arrives at unbelief in the strict sense.
7. Rejection of a personal God, either through agnostic
   suspension of judgement, or atheistic denial of his existence.
8. Apathy over all religious questioning—religious indifference in its fullest sense of a complete absence of interest in the possibility of faith.

From this schema it is clear that one cannot simply identify non-
practice with non-belief, and yet the abandonment of practice can
be a key step in the direction of a deeper confusion over faith, and
eventual loss.

A key question is how quickly a person passes through these
various stages. While there are no hard and fast certainties here, it
is clear that it depends on the society one has grown up within. In
cultures, like Ireland and Quebec, which were strongly church-
centred and placed a lot of emphasis on Sunday practice, a person
may move more rapidly down the scale. If external practice has

played a dominant role as an expression of religious commitment, its abandonment will leave the greater void. It has been estimated that in the case of a person for whom practice was previously their principal form of religion, four years of non-practice could easily add up to practical unbelief, and they would be likely to find themselves somewhere in the second half of the schema. If this is true, then it puts a question mark against the more optimistic hypothesis, that religious faith can often continue in individuals despite decline of practice. Certainly this could be true of a number of conscientious searchers, but the majority of people will be more likely to fall victim to the prevailing drift. Two opposite errors must be avoided: either putting so much emphasis on practice that one reduces Christianity to ritual performance, or being so dismissive of the importance of regular community worship as to underestimate its crucial role in supporting the faith of most people.

It helps to see clearly the various phases that a person may go through, between beginning to abandon church practice and arriving at unbelief. These stages can also be rooted in different inner moods, and indeed it is often easy to forget the influence of these psychological states on what we think are rational decisions.

It is worth recalling the crucial role played by a person's basic attitude, in any journey towards faith or away from it. Cardinal Newman once remarked, with his usual lucidity, that "with good dispositions faith is easy" but "without good dispositions faith is not easy". It is of the very nature of decisions over religion that they are not a matter of pure reason, that they can involve a strong element of a person's general feeling about themselves and about existence.

Before outlining some interesting psychological research done in Montreal on this area, let me begin with a true story of a meeting I had with a university student some years back, and which has since become a parable for me, revealing something of the role of emotions in conclusions about faith. One day a student was discussing his essay with me when, out of the blue, he announced in a pretty aggressive manner, "I'm an atheist, you know". I paid no attention and continued to comment on his essay. "Isn't it your job to try and convert me?" he asked. "I wouldn't dream of converting anyone in that tone of voice", I found myself saying, and went on to explain that faith was something precious to me, too precious to have a futile argument about. If he was willing to listen, some other time I would try to tell him what it meant to me. That was that for the moment.

He came back a few days later, saying that he wanted to talk things over. The tone was a bit tense, but his very coming back said a lot. He started by announcing that there was something difficult he had to tell me about himself. He beat around the bush a little, then said, "I suffer from asthma". I thought this was an introduction to something bigger, but no: it was almost the whole story. Thank God I didn't laugh. Because asthma had ruined his childhood, had cut him off from a lot of life, and became something he was ashamed of, and deeply angry over. Cutting the story short for now, that day I had an important insight, and I now assume that behind many an aggressive rejection ("I'm an atheist") there can live a softer reality of disappointment or hurt ("I suffer from asthma"). Not of course that I want to deny the possibility of mature and conscious unbelief, but I think it is rare.

One does not have to be much of a psychologist to discern that my student's unbelief had much more to do with his own experience of life, than with any purely religious conclusions.

Because of what he had gone through, it was only too easy to awaken a whole cluster of negative emotions towards himself, towards others, and towards God too. This can be true in less dramatic ways of many other seemingly rational forms of unbelief, and of course there can also be immature forms of faith, sadly shaped by fears and resentments. The thesis of the three A's has been mentioned already—the division of types of unbelief into three families, alienation, anger and apathy. If we probe a little deeper we will find very different emotions underlying these three attitudes.

Leopold de Reyes has worked on this whole question in Montreal, and has found the psychological insights of "transactional analysis" to be particularly enlightening. What this school has popularised under the title of *I'm OK, You're OK* can be brought to bear on the progression of inner states that underlie different types of unbelief.

If that slogan represents the ideal positive attitude towards oneself and others, three negative variants are possible as

illustrated in the accompanying diagram. It seems helpful to identify the different versions of unbelief in terms of underlying moods
and emotions. This is not to reduce unbelief or explain it away, but
simply to claim that a purely intellectual rejection of religion is
rare, and that more often than not, an unbeliever will show some
signs of these negative feelings. (Needless to say they are also part
of the experience of the believer, but he or she manages to arrive at
a different decision in response to them). What this diagram suggests is that various experiences of relationship toward God or
Church can arouse various negative reactions. In particular it may
induce fear, or hostility or indifference.

Another implication—indicated by the arrows—is that there
may be a natural progression towards a more mature faith that goes
through precisely those three states of negativity. The journey
through alienation and anger and apathy could become stuck at
any one point, or it could be a fruitful and purifying journey
towards an adult decision for faith. This too is embodied in the
diagram in the dotted line: underneath that line is largely passive,
and deals with what happens to people, often unconsciously; above
that line is the positive relationship, that does not simply happen
but has to be chosen.

Thus, the diagram and its underlying psychological theory
helps to suggest not only that there may be a very different set of attitudes linked with the three main families of unbelief, but also that
the journey to faith may well involve a passage through negatives,
to positive choices about God or church. Once again the point is
emphasised that faith has to be a decision, and that many forms of
unbelief may be forms of non-decision.

All this is offered in the hope that it helps towards seeing more
clearly the hidden personal factors that can often be present in
unbelief. In fact it could be looked upon as an up-dating of the old
spiritual wisdom of discernment. At the core of this tradition was the
golden rule: never make any change when in a state of desolation.
Translated into our more modern terms and applied to the area of
belief and unbelief, it might be expanded in a few steps as follows:

1. Recognise that you may be acting from unrecognised
    negative emotions, and they in turn may be rooted in
    various hurts that have little to do with the world of faith.

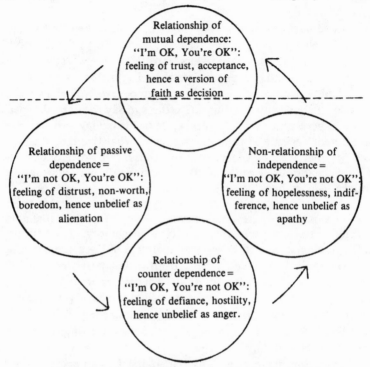

2. If this true, go further and pinpoint your typical cluster of negative emotions; you will probably find that they fall into one or other of the families mentioned—fear, hostility, indifference.

3. Beware of allowing these hidden moods to influence your search for faith; if they are present, you can only make a bad decision: so simply wait through the storm, faithful to what once made sense.

4. It is only when you are in a state of inner freedom and positively disposed towards yourself and life that you are ripe for any important decision. (Indeed the same would apply to marriage decisions, or any of the crucial steps in life's journey).

So it is an important skill of wisdom to be able to distinguish the true self from the false self in one's daily flux of moods: and it has immense bearing on the question of options for or against faith. When the false self is in the driving seat, only poor results can be expected. When the true self is present, new wisdom is possible.

6

THE IMPACT OF SOCIAL CHANGE

Whàt happens to religious awareness in a period of huge cultural change? The Marxists like to say that context conditions consciousness, in the sense that the socio-economic environment determines in many ways how people think and feel and imagine their lives. Faith has to do with imagining and feeling and thinking about God. It involves believing and belonging, the possibility of both of these must be deeply influenced by new social situations and lifestyles. Let us take Ireland as a revealing example of the impact of such social change.

A new era of Irish Catholicism was ushered in within a few months of the late fifties. In the autumn of 1958 Pope Pius XII died and was succeeded by John XXIII: it was the end of a certain style of authoritative church leadership and the inauguration of a new openness that was to lead to the Second Vatican Council. Then, in the summer of 1959, Ireland saw a not dissimilar transition of power with the retirement from active government of Eamon de Valera (on his election as President), and the choice of Sean Lemass as his successor.

In Dublin, as in the Vatican, a shift of values was taking place, and both were to have profound consequences. The old language of Irish nationalism was not altogether abandoned, but a quiet revolution happened whereby economics became the dominant value in Irish politics. And this in turn laid the foundation for a most successful industrial expansion and the newly affluent Irish society that evolved for most people in the sixties. Clearly this new phenomenon of widespread and relatively rapid social change would have an unsettling effect on religious values. Some two centuries ago, John Wesley remarked that "wherever riches have increased, the essence of religion has decreased in the same proportion".

One relatively simple way of approaching this area is by mens of diagram. In situation A, society is largely traditional and nonurban, as was the case in Ireland until the early sixties, and it may still be the case in villages and smaller communities. In this pre-1958 situation the Church tended to be dominant, in a good sense, in people's lives. It was naturally at the centre of local life, and insofar as there was any unbelief it was usually a matter of eccentric individuals who fell out with the Church for some reason, or voiced doubts about the whole business of faith.

Three situations for faith

	A	B	C
KIND OF SOCIETY	Stable, rural; older culture of obedience; protected world	New affluence, media exposure; mobility of values	Urban non-community: technological, complex, class divided
POSITION OF CHURCH	Dominant, central institutional authority	Religion as one influence among others; more autonomy for human values	A marginal institution; relativity of world-views
TYPE OF "UNBELIEF" FOUND	Non-practice by marginal individuals	Alienation of sub-groups from inherited religion (youth, workers etc.)	Widespread indifference; eclipse of sense of God
LANGUAGE OF FAITH	Belong to deep convention rooted in sacraments	Struggle for personal conviction, rooted in relationship to Christ	Option for different way of life; rooted in search for community and for justice
PASTORAL RESPONSES	Bring individuals back to sacraments	Renew church structures for better evangelization (small communities)	Critique of society; awaken basic question of God

Such non-conformists would be looked upon as odd by most people. Then the typical reaction of priests was to encourage them back to the sacraments, and one may recall the role of the parish mission of the forties or fifties in this respect.

I have memories of visiting members of religious orders parading up the village street to call upon those who did not come to Mass; an encounter took place which the Vatican Council might not recognise as dialogue with non-believers. But in those days the desired result might well ensue, and the village deviants might return to the fold for a time.

That is one way of viewing the first column of the diagram, dealing with Situation A. But the assumptions of that world have disappeared—or have they? There is always the possibility of people continuing the thinking and methods of Situation A when in fact they are being challenged by Situation B. And there can be little doubt that the process begun in Ireland, in 1958-1959, has inevitably spelt the death of A and the emergence of B. With the increasing urbanisation and industry, with more wealth and education (however unevenly divided), with the more pluralist values assimilated from the media, it seems clear that for the most part Ireland is either at an early or late stage of B, depending on where one lives.

Turning then to the contrasting characteristics sketched in the second column, obviously the most important change is that the individual-centred analysis and response of A is no longer adequate. The assumptions of the fifties no longer apply, and one is now aware of whole groups of people who become alienated from the practice of religion. As mentioned earlier, the Young Urban Male is a sub-group very clearly in crisis.

Another grouping showing signs of collective withdrawal from practice would be the younger married couples in city housing estates. At all events the phenomenon of non-practice at this stage is no longer a matter of marginal individuals, but of significant minorities. Moreover, behind this external decline in practice can lie a new crisis of diminishing faith. Many new questions of pastoral interpretation arise. Some would blame this secularisation process for bringing about the eclipse of a sense of God; others would query whether the image of God had not been impoverished in the first place. Could it be that the new outer pressures are bringing into the open the immaturities of religion as understood in Situation A?

At all events the pastoral reactions of those who recognise the newness of B tend to be difficult in focus: they give priority to evangelisation over sacraments, and they tend to prefer the smaller community to the big church as the best setting for the communication of faith. In this respect one thinks of the great variety of smaller growth groups that have burgeoned in recent years, all endeavouring to build up communities of faith-support within the larger non-community.

It seems unlikely that any parts of Ireland are yet within the context envisaged by Situation C. Any church that is worried when its teenagers' practice declines from seventy-eight per cent to sixty-four per cent can hardly be described as "a marginal institution". Where Situation C exists, whether Manchester, Marseilles, Munich or Milan, even a half of those percentages would be looked on as a great achievement. Situation C refers to a secular society of long standing, where practical unbelief on a massive scale is inherited (no matter what people may say when asked whether they believe in God), and where church-going is culturally unthinkable for most people, most of the time. As to responses, the diagram suggests a two-tiered strategy. On the one hand the Church has the prophetic call to voice its criticism of the dehumanising effects of this environment, and its preaching role will focus no longer on evangelisation in the first place (much less on sacraments), but rather on ways of arousing the basic religious hunger that can be smothered in such a society. Of course there is no need to await the arrival of C before these goals become relevant in pastoral work.

As well as clarifying the vastly different context for the struggle of faith and the typical forms of unbelief this diagram may prove useful in another respect. A, B and C can indicate not simply external or sociological situations, but also inner languages of understanding that different people can assume to be credible. Many parents, whose upbringing was in the fifties or before, will naturally be people of Situation A, and its language may be in their blood and bones. The type of religion that is normally assumed in A is strong on obedience and authority: "you do what the Church says". The natural mode of discourse is either imperative or else exhortation; in both cases the assumption is that one person knows better and the other person should listen and obey.

In short, one can have a source of much pain and confused communication between generations on this point. Where parents use the inherited language of A, and where older children automatically speak the language of B, then there can be a chasm of misunderstanding and hurt. The language of B is much more rooted in the validity of personal experience rather than in unquestioning acceptance of norms. So it is vital to recognise a huge shift in the "plausibility structures" between one kind of society and the other: where faith could assume the support of a stable society in the fifties and before, that is not so any longer.

Indeed the emergence of the so-called "youth culture" of the sixties and later would have been unthinkable in Situation A: no wonder its language is often found incomprehensible by those who have never left the inner language of A behind.

The purpose of this discussion has been to stress the radical nature of social change and its crucial influence on people's religious attitudes. It is not so much that a new and complex way of life automatically promotes unbelief; rather it means the likely demise of a certain kind of faith, and the need for a different kind of rootedness. In the words of Karl Rahner,

> Our faith was partially and essentially
> conditioned by a quite different sociological
> situation which at that time supported us and
> which today does not exist.

The result is that the context of faith is significantly different as a society moves from A to B; in particular, faith has now to be more or a decision than an inheritance, and a decision often against the tide. This new situation need not be hostile to faith, as such, but only to a more passive form of faith. Providentially this situation can bring about a purifying of faith; or, to adapt the image at the heart of the parable of the sower, if in Situation A it was enough to sow the seed of faith two inches down and it came to fruit, in Situation B that same seed will need to be sown four inches down; not because the seed itself is weaker: the Gospel remains the same; but conditions above the ground are more stormy and the environment immensely more difficult for growth.

7

TYPES OF UNBELIEF

So far we have looked at unbelief from three angles: the stages it often goes through, the subjective feelings that can underlie it and the social contexts that also influence this. This section will examine the different ways in which people objectify their rejection of faith. In each instance the question will be "what seems to be the most likely root of this form of unbelief?"

Although there is a danger of oversimplification, it can help to divide the many types of unbelief into three principal families, at least from the point of view of their origins. Some unbelievers claim that their main reason for finding faith impossible lies in the area of *conscious thinking;* they come to the conclusion that God cannot exist. Another group of unbelievers take a different line: for them the emphasis is more on *conscious* or *unconsicous choosing* of an interpretation of life that has no need for God, whether or not he exists. And a third type consists in a more *unconscious passivity;* these are unbelievers who tend to drift with the crowd or with the times, and therefore are often less articulate in giving reasons for their attitude.

First Family

Typical expressions of the thought-out rejection of God would go something like this:

I'm trained as a scientist—I can't swallow such a fairy tale on such slender evidence.

The more one knows about the way the gospels were written, the more likely it is that they imagined the Resurrection.

It's Christians who are incredible; if God existed, his so-called followers would show it.

The word "God" is so slippery: either it's too neat and cheap, or else it fades into being something meaningless; we can't talk about it at all.

There's more than enough to get on with in the world I can see and experience.

Isn't it a Santa Claus situation? People imagine someone to befriend them—and so religion is childish make-believe.

Something spiritual yes, within me, possibly beyond me, but I can't make sense of a personal God.

These colloquial and often-heard expressions of unbelief are variants on two of the great traditions of atheism in Western thought: all materialist, empiricist forms of thought, which assume that any mystery beyond the senses is impossible to apprehend; and secondly, the more psychological analysis that dismiss faith as projection of false human hopes. This whole family of unbelief is more usual in educationally advanced individuals and groups; indeed it often stems from the fact that a person's intellectual grasp of the foundations of faith may have fallen disastrously behind their level of expertise in some professional area. It can also result from a failure of religious education to be a genuine formation of the mind, or from a wider and deeper failure of the Church over a few generations to find ways of communicating faith in the languages of new and complex culture. But of course these difficulties of the intellect over faith can also be purifying reminders of the darkness of any human knowledge of God.

Second Family

Those whose unbelief is rooted in some kind of choice belong to the family called atheism-by-reaction. Even though they may often give reasoned arguments for their position, the deeper roots involve negative experiences of one kind or another. As Karl Rahner has put it:

> The real argument against Christianity is this experience of darkness. I have always found that behind the technical arguments levelled against Christianity... there are always various experiences of life causing the spirit and the heart to be dark, tired and despairing.

Rahner seems to imply that a pure unbelief of conscious thought is rare and that it is at least linked with some attitude of the will, if not in fact inspired by that attitude. Let us voice some of the familiar forms in which this version of unbelief might express itself:

I see too much suffering around, completely innocent suffering, to be able to make any sense of a good God who is meant to be all-powerful.

Just look at the history of religions and how they bring about wars; religion has done more harm than good to humanity.

The only God most people seem to find is one that lets them off the hook of their own responsibility: pie in the sky means they do nothing about changing this world now.

My religious upbringing only damaged me, left me with scars and hangovers of guilt.

The day primitive man cooked up the idea of some god beyond him was a degrading day for humanity, it gave shape to his capacity to live from fear instead of from freedom.

I can't really accept the Great Answerer of my little petitions, and not only because he seems permanently on strike.

The Church bit turns me off entirely; I didn't want Sunday ruined by bad sermons, boredom and just general annoyance.

Underlying all these expressions of unbelief is one recurring motif: a sense at least of disappointment and woundedness or even of horror over some evil. The evil may be seen in others, in oneself, or in the influence of religion in society. One may be clearly conscious of its impact or else only vaguely aware of something wrong somewhere. But in each case there is a response, involving emotions and will, that feels forced to reject faith. It is not enough to sidestep these accusing voices by supposing that they attack only false gods, or by regretting that some people will inevitably get the wrong impression of faith or of religion. This family of unbelief, by often irate reaction, can be saying something true about the falsity of believers, and, indeed, about the sheer difficulty of authentic faith. Thus, it becomes clear that the very existence of this type of unbelief can offer a prophetic protest against frequently accepted, but inadequate, images of God, and equally against impoverished forms of religion in practice.

Third Family

Another category of unbelief is more social and cultural in its roots. It is immediately rooted in some situation of change as outlined earlier in this section in our ABC diagram. It is less a matter of conscious reflection or of reflections and choices, and much more a question of people being carried along by prevailing influences. God is not rejected but he becomes gradually eclipsed: literally, other things get in the way and block out the possibility of faith. And so the expressions of this kind of unbelief are characteristically less definite and more confused than were the other two families:

I don't know really; religion sort of faded out for me after school and I never bothered much with it since.

Perhaps there is a God but I leave all that to church people—it never grabbed me.

I'm always saying I'd like to work out the meaning of life again but I never seem to have time for it.

Sure, I keep up the church-going I was brought up with; I wouldn't like to say why, or what I get out of it. It doesn't do me any harm: maybe it doesn't do me any good either.

Religion is all right for special occasions but it's out of touch with experience; the way we live now, God is unreal most of the time.

There's too much to sort out; I don't know how anyone could feel certain enought to say they believe any more.

The tone of these statements is more one of sadness or unsureness than of any anger or strong denial of God. They were rooted in two linked experiences of modern life: the crowded consciousness of mankind stimulated either with crippling complexity or superficial excitements, and the sense of a yawning gap between the world of faith and the world of the everyday. They stem from people being vaguely aware of frustration in their natural religious search; they seem locked in a state of mind and incapable of breaking out. In this why they are more victims than choosers, even though one must also admit the possibility of a careless type of unbeliever, one who allows faith to languish from sheer laziness and disinterest.

A pessimistic analysis of this whole situation would say that it is no more than the reverse of the coin of conventional church adherence in the past: where one used to have passive but shallow belief, now one has passive but shallow unbelief. It is simply the tide that has changed, so that those who were previously drifting in one direction are now going a different way. But once again a more challenging interpretation is possible: just as the two previous types of unbelief could be seen as truth-bringers that could in fact purify faith, so too, the present indifference to faith is a call to move beyond convention to conviction and commitment—as we shall see in our third part.

8

A CONVERGENCE OF CAUSES

An earlier chapter looked at the more open approach to atheism initiated at Vatican II. In the twenty years or so since that happened, much has changed. In particular the issue of unbelief is seen less as an atheism of the intellect alone and much more as an apathy or indifference towards religion. The agenda has broadened, so to speak, from thinking of atheism as a crisis of meaning to looking on the many forms of unbelief as part of a larger crisis in culture as a whole.

It is also becoming clear that there can be no one simple explanation of the phenomenon of unbelief today. To begin with, we become aware of the very different faces of what may only loosely be called unbelief. And so to gather together the insights of these last sections, let us try to see the causes of unbelief today in terms of a convergence of four factors.

This can be presented in terms of a clash between new and old, a clash that spells more a crisis of culture than of faith in itself. It is a story of two dramatically new forces meeting with two more conservative and unchanging factors. On the one hand we have the emergence of a radically new way of living, accompanied by a whole new cluster of ideas and attitudes. On the other hand we have the Church as cautious and slow to move, and families and individuals often unready for the business of finding their bearings in this new world.

The first factor is only another version of the social change diagram already discussed. One has only to recall family life before the advent of television to have a concrete example of a small, but significant, change in most people's experience of home. Added to that would be the much greater mobility and the fact that the entertainment industry has become so immensely expanded, and found a ripe market in a more moneyed youth.

What emerges is a picture of uprooting of many traditional ways of relating within families and the dominance of a new culture, one that thrives on continual stimulus and leaves little space for stillness. Clearly this has enormous impact on the religious dimension, especially among the younger generation, and there is no point in merely lamenting the fact, or hoping that the clock would in some way be turned backwards. As always, what is required is recognition of the new dangers and then response to the new challenges. The dangers on the level of life-style are that the religious sense may be ousted from people's consciousness, and that the consumerist pressures keep mystery at bay, so aborting the innate religious search of each person before it can come to fruit. Indeed, alternative gods are provided: success, sport, sex, security in superficial ways. As one Nobel prize-winner has put it, "the world is too much with us, and there has never been so much world".

As summarised in the diagram here, life-style is only one strand of at least four influences, promoting a climate where unbelief becomes much more likely than before. A new philosophy of life can be found at the heart of modern culture, and one that quietly displaces the older-religious perspectives from the centre of the stage. Within less than a generation a radically new humanism has had immense impact, even on many people who would not know what that term meant. The ideology implicit in all the public domains of life, from places of work to places of entertainment, has become naturally and entirely human-centred. The world is self-sufficient, and runs its business in so highly efficient a way that it leaves little time for any other horizons.

To take one simple example, when I was a student in University College, Dublin, around 1960, an amazing scene took place every day in the library at noon: everyone there stood and in silence said the Angelus. Even a Buddhist girl from Thailand whom I knew quite well stood in silence. I would love to know when exactly the custom died, but I know that now it would be unthinkable for anyone to make such a public gesture; I wouldn't do it myself. A mere twenty years ago only a brave crack-pot would sit down; now only a brave crack-pot would stand up. A different ethos is dominant, which entails the retreat of religion to a largely personal domain. Does it go further than this and become a narrowing of faith into the merely private?

Although the world of religion is still a central and accepted part of life it can become reduced to a pale and unreal realm by the implicit doctrines of the practical worlds of business, technology, communications, and even of education when competitively inter-preted. Faced with this "real world", impoverished images of an unreal God become even more unreal and thin.

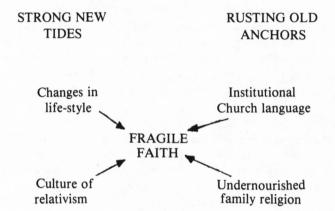

Another aspect of a humanist culture deserves mention, even if briefly: people are exposed to the tower of Babel of the modern in-tellectual world even through popular media such as television debates. A mere rumour that faith is not credible any more can be disturbing to people poorly equipped to think such arguments through. In the same way, an exposure to conflicting moral values can leave people deeply confused and a prey to relativism.

A particular form of unbelief that comes from this new culture is what can be called the "threshold stance", and it is one that seems uniquely prevalent among the younger generation in the West in recent years. It is less an attitude of rejection as of non-acceptance, of inability to cross the threshold into some level of commitment. There can be a considerable respect for genuinely religious people, or a reverence for the person of Jesus, or a certain spiritual search for ways of meditation; but the journey stops short of any "yes" that lasts.

I recall one student who spent a long time on a quest for some

religious anchor in his life. There was a period of many questions
and of many ups and downs of moods. At times the whole effort
seemed pointless to him. His breakthrough came in two classic
moments, with some weeks in between.

The first involved his discovery of a "sense of sin", when instead of equating sin with sins and so listing the more obvious guilts
and falls of each life, he actually had an insight into the frightening
selfishness of his whole attitude and of the dividedness of his heart.
This was a moment of liberation. A second such moment came with
similar pain: it was when he discovered that to commit himself to
Christianity was what he called a "huge step"; for his normal self it
would be a revolution. In fact, with much unsureness along the
way, this man was eventually able to cross the threshold into that
rare "yes" to Christ. But this meant listening to, and yet overcom-
ing, the sceptical and dubious voices of the culture all around him;
for the whole impact of that culture is usually towards Perhaps
rather than Yes or No. There are so many unanswered questions
that they come to be seen as unanswerable. To continue some form
of searching seems more honest than to decide on what seems just
one answer. The very complexity of the culture seems to make
definite commitments look like easy answers, answers that are at
least premature, it not incredible.

Over against this new world shaped by a life-style and a cluster
of attitudes that were unheard of a mere twenty years ago, there
stands a somewhat worried and uncertain Church, itself composed
of individuals most of whom would be more at home in the conventional religion born of a stable society. It could be said of the
Church as an institution that she too would be more at home in
Situation A, because it is a fairly new experience for her to cope
with a state of continual flux.

To put the matter in oversimplified form, if the world has now
entered a dramatic evolution of life-styles and of attitudes, the
danger is that the Church and believers may pull back into a new
ghetto mentality where they listen only to themselves. That would
be a serious failure of missionary nerve, through opting however
unconsciously, to remain within the "railings". It would also be a
pastoral tragedy, because in the long term it would mean abandoning those on the margins of church belonging to their fate of drifting towards unbelief.

But this is to speak in a future or conditional tense. There is the more immediate question of how the Church may have already contributed to the decline of faith, and the slide towards unbelief. In earlier pages we have seen to what extent Ireland's brand of unbelief takes the shape of alienation from the externals of the Church. There is nothing new in people being critical of aspects of Church life. One has only to recall the image of religion emerging from many Irish writers to realise that the clerical church was often viewed as domineering, insensitive and even hypocritical.

What is new, however, in the last decade or so, is that this critique is no longer confined to a few literary people but can be echoed in different ways by whole groups of the younger generation. The point is not whether the accusations are justified; the fact is that the church has acquired the "image of a sterile institution" in the eyes of many younger people (the phrase comes from the Irish National Conference of Priests as far back as 1978). Although the social scene has drastically changed, the mainstream of church activity seems geared to those still living from Situation A; it seems to give priority to maintenance over mission. And for the younger mentality, deeply shaped by the assumptions of Situation B, a religion of mere piety or of mere obligation appears to be a sham.

In the eyes of many of the younger generation the church experience is thin and lacking in any depth; allied to this is the fact that the church institution is viewed with eyes of suspicion. The credibility crisis here is only part of a much longer crisis of authority in our culture. The young have come to be profoundly sceptical of any authority that relies on its own authority to justify itself. Thus "the Church teaches" is somewhat of a red rag to the bull, evoking many versions of "why". The formula for danger here lies in the coming together of a poor level of experience and an unconvincing language of authority. Indeed, it is a classic case of a clash between the accepted values of Situation A and Situation B. A tends to rely on obedience and to have little sensitivity to the nebulous level of how things are experienced. But B is quite the opposite: it trusts the horizon of relationship and experience as central, and remains cold and unimpressed by appeals to a more central authority.

The growing irrelevance of conventional church activities in the eyes of those living today's new culture is a third major source favourable to unbelief. In 1975, the Vatican Secretariat for Non-Believers launched a worldwide inquiry into just this area, seeing the crisis as more connected with the meditations of faith through Church than as one of faith itself. The initial document announcing the survey spoke in fairly blunt terms:

> We accept as a fact that, in Europe, many young people are living a strictly marginal Christianity. with no understanding of it, nor any desire to learn about it. Many of these young people, born into Christian families and baptised, are abandoning not only the sacramental practice of their faith but the faith itself.

And the subsequent reports did not mince their words:

> The change between generations may be of a new order: there are now no elders who know more than the young themselves about what the young are experiencing...
>
> What the Church is up against is a generation that is by no means sure it has a future...
> Just as the Church is pessimistic towards youth, so is youth pessimistic about the Church...
> Questions on the unbelief of the young require that one should also ask about the credibility of the Church.

What emerges then is not simply critique of the Church for the sake of critique, but rather for the sake of renewed relevance in her central mission. It is also apparent that (to adapt the words of Vatican II) the Church itself "can have more than a little to do" with the birth of unbelief. In particular, this is a problem of communication and of priorities.

Of communication: because when a generation feel themselves both unheard and unspoken to, they can only experience distance and disinterest.

Of priorities: because it is a typical church-centred temptation to invest time and effort in familiar patterns, at the expense of more difficult pastoral contacts. A church that seems indifferent to those who begin to feel indifferent can only confirm their indifference.

The fourth and final source of unbelief that I want to suggest concerns the family, and indeed, the general unpreparedness of people to cope with the complexity of today's world as an environment for faith. I should make it clear that I am not accusing the family of being a deliberate source of unbelief (any more than the Church itself); it is much more a question of lacks rather than conscious failures here. But let me begin with a concrete observation from my own pastoral experience. I have yet to come across a fully unbelieving university student who had a good relationship with believing parents. Clearly I should explain what those words mean as it seems a strong claim.

By "fully unbelieving" I mean not just someone non-practising, but one who seems to have closed the door on God in a permanent fashion.

By "good relationship" I mean not just peaceful co-existence or the absence of major friction, but a fairly sustained effort on the part of the parents to alter their wavelength of communication as the child grew towards adulthood, and perhaps (but not always possible) towards some explicit sharing of faith within the family.

By "believing" I would mean that the parents themselves avoid the trap for faith in a married context: that of falling into the rut of non-growth, of remaining at a level of pious but conventional belonging to the Church.

The faith that is not as articulate as other values in one's life will fade into unaliveness in today's pressurised context. And it seems to be a sad fate of many married couples to set out with high hopes of being good Christian parents, but to undermine their own hopes by not taking the necessary steps to nourish their own faith. That undernourished faith may well survive for them, because its roots are deep. But in a very real way, that manlnutrition may prove contagious for their children; the message they may receive is that although faith is very important for their parents it remains an external tradition, a matter of conformism with some prayer behind it. Although the parents have genuine faith, however weakened through non-growth, what may easily be communicated non-verbally to the children is something not worth growing into.

The claim being made here is that because of a new cultural context, the family has become the crucial battle-ground where the struggle for faith is either won or lost. One could even argue that the pressures of new life-styles are superficial by comparison wito the deep influence of the home, and that likewise, the impact of the Church (or the school) is quite secondary to the day-to-day communication of values within the family circle.

Some parents react to such statements with a certain impatience, and accuse us (teachers, priests, religious, etc) of passing the buck once the going gets hot. Of course there can be some truth there, but in fact it is because the going has got hot that the family has to recognise its role at the centre of the stage for the transmission of faith. It was always there, but did not have to be so conscious of its role in a Situation A. Now that the tide has changed, the family is the main place to learn to swim against the tide; to keep that metaphor, the school and the Church can usually only improve on the basic skill of swimming learned in the family. If this picture is correct, it means that malnutrition or mediocrity of faith within the family can cause a silent, but sinister, erosion of faith in the next generation.

In St Luke's gospel (chapter 14) there is a parable of planning, one of the lesser known of the stories of Jesus. It tells of a man who set out to build a tower but forgot to count how many bricks he would need; he gets half-way and then has to leave a jagged and unfinished edifice. And we are told people looking on will laugh at him for not having worked out his requirements in advance. In the same place is the parallel parable of going to war without having knowledge of the enemy's strength. As we come to the close of Part II of this book, our journey could be seen in terms of those parables. Part I sought to reconnoitre the potentially threatening pressures against faith today. Part II has inquired more about new weakness in our readiness to confront these dangers, and about why the war situation has arisen at all. Part III will attempt an architect's first draft for the tower that is now required.

PART THREE

Responses

As promised in the preface, this third section moves on to a difficult and more ambitious task: it dares suggest ways of answering some of the issues surveyed in the two earlier parts. The first piece envisages four concerned believers coming together to consider the challenges to faith today and finding that they have four rather different sets of assumptions about how it should be tackled. This imagined conversation is placed first in order to highlight the painful but also fruitful divergences that people can have when faced with this new religious situation. Next, there follows a batch of three short essays directed to groups in the frontline of any pastoral response to unbelief among youth: priests (a fantasy speech on their possible programme in religious education); and parents (a letter addressed to those worried about their childrens' non-practice). After this comes a further trio of letters intended for young adults and singling out three individuals: one an undernourished adherent to religious practice, one lapsed, and one more fully unbelieving. These letters are based on real people but any identifying features have been left out. As this whole section progresses, it shifts from a largely church rooted language about renewal of faith to some attempt to reach out to those distanced from the world of official religion. The final pages are couched in a more exploratory and personal vein, and seek to sketch a new relationship between believer and non-believer in our time.

9

A QUARTET OF BELIEVERS—ON THE FUTURE OF FAITH

This section stems largely from discussions and question sessions that I have participated in with many people in recent years. Gradually it came home to me that there exists a considerable variety of approaches to the faith situation now. More than that, it seemed that the differences of viewpoint were rooted in quite different assumptions about the nature of church or faith or today's world. In short, the differences on the level of response stemmed from differing theological stances. Reflecting on this, it came home to me that even in the New Testament one discovers a wide spectrum of emphasis on faith. The divergent temperaments of Peter and Paul are well known, Peter being the cautious leader, filled with pastoral care of the flock, and Paul the more vehement evangelist of the pagans. But if Paul stresses the impact of faith in Christ on a personal basis, James seems to put his emphasis slightly differently — "faith without works is dead". Putting all this in drastically simple form, one can see even in the New Testament a divergence of understandings of the nature of religion: where Peter would be the man of the institution, Paul would be the missioner and evangelist, and James would be the liberation theologian, with his focus on commitment in action. These creative tensions seem echoed in today's discussions except that one major voice is not included—the voice of the woman—and the voice that can also ponder the special traits of our present faith situation. Historical consciousness was not part of the New Testament. And so I have added the voice of Martha, as representing another horizon, and as rooting herself in the experiential level of today's world.

The reader is asked to suspend dramatic judgement and to take these pages as illustrating the fruitful variety of lights and gifts that make up our Church at the moment. The scene is Peter's house. He is a hard-working priest in a parish. He has decided to have an evening of reflection with three invited guests. Martha is a wife and

mother of four children, ranging from fifteen to twenty-four. Paul
is a priest, involved mainly in youth ministry through school
retreats and the like. James is a committed Christian who is a social
worker in an inner city area.

Peter opened the discussion by voicing his worries about the
survival of faith and, he outlined two hypotheses about the future.
Either the continuation of a people's Church is still possible or it is
not. The optimistic view is to work for the preservation of faith and
church practice by the vast majority of people. A darker prediction
would suggest that as we move towards the year 2000 the trend will
be for a deeper loss of contact and of credibility by church institutions. Against this background Peter invites the reactions of his
guests.

Our eavesdropping on their conversations begins at a moment
when Martha is warming to her theme of the new texture to life today, and how this shapes a different context for faith.

Martha:
Perhaps what I have to offer is peculiarly a woman's intuition; certainly it stems from my sense of what is happening to people in
their personal experience. I'm talking about the impact of a quiet
cultural revolution on most of the new generation. When the Pope
was in Ireland he used a phrase that spoke volumes to me: he said
that each generation was like a "new continent" to be won for
Christ. That sums up for me the radicalness of the break between
generations today. For most people over forty the semi-conscious
assumptions about life are in an older mould; they respect obedience, authority, duty; they think of themselves as adhering to a
church institution that "knows better", and while they may not
always agree, mostly they listen with respect. Their's is an obedience culture. But the young have an experience culture. Things do
not become acceptable because authority has said so; the relationship, as experienced, is crucial. So they give out about the Church
in many ways, but none more seriously than in the human dimension of its relationship to them. They complain that it is imper-
sonal, boring, bossy, conventional. By this they mean the atmosphere of non-community which they experience on Sunday.
And they also judge priests to be merely institutional men. The
same is often felt and said by the older generation as well, but (and

it is a crucial "but"), they do not therefore make the same break with the Church. The culture of obedience can survive a certain level of human inadequacy, but the culture of experience is inclined to allow little room for something that does not speak to them strongly or deeply.

Paul:
I like that analysis. I accept that something of that gulf of different expectations exists. And therefore I see the young as hungry for a non-institutional experience of church and of faith. Here lies the vast importance of the small growth groups that I was advocating earlier. Yes, I think Martha has put her finger on something of central importance in understanding the background to the struggle for faith today. It's like my namesake in the New Testament, having his intuition into the totally different needs of the Gentiles on their journey to Christ; a journey that should not be thought of as if they were Jews. The Jews were an obedience culture, people of strong inheritance. The Gentiles needed to be convinced by very different approaches.

James:
Martha's insight is attractive to me too, because it allows for the wider world, wider than the merely individual. She is saying, or at least implying, that the individual in search for faith today is conditioned in a totally different way from thirty years ago. But where Martha seems to speak of this mainly as a problem, I think of it also as a huge potential. This new culture is much more alert, not only to experience, but also to society, and to the world society. They are much less likely to be satisfied by a merely private faith. This seems to me to be one reason why they are "turned off" by the conventional Sunday duty. The worst thing about it is that it becomes totally unchallenging, just a pious exercise (poor on the level of human experience as Martha says) but worse still, one that seems to have no impact on the real life of our time. I remember sitting in a university restaurant once at lunch time, and from where I was eating with a friend we could see a long queue of students coming to eat. The queue died out and then, suddenly, it started again as a substantial new group arrived, some two hundred or so. My friend asked where they all came from. From daily Mass during

Lent, I replied. Do that many go to Mass every day? My surprised
friend made a memorable remark: if the communists had two hundred at a meeting every day, we'd soon hear from them. His remark
set met thinking about the unchallenging cosiness of liturgy in
general.

My hunch is that the younger generation find public worship
empty because it is poorly prayed and non-existent as an experience
of community, but most of all because it fails to be a source of mission in society.

Peter:
That sounds marvellous, but where would you even begin? You're
living in an imaginary world if you think that the crowded church
on Sunday can somehow become a place of warm community, or
of social awareness leading to action. You seem to have no idea of
the limitations of time and freedom within a fairly rushed forty-five
minutes.

James:
But that's what we are beginning to question: whether the crowded
church on Sunday can be the central event of our religion in any
real sense for today. Martha would say no, because the big church
is inevitably too anonymous and thin as experience. Paul would say
no, because he's very keen on the small groups as sources of a more
committed faith. And I too say no, because unless the gathering for
the Eucharist can be a genuine stimulus to a change of life and a
deepening of commitment, I think it is a dangerously narrowed
practice of the meaning of the Last Supper.

Peter:
So you don't see the Sunday, as we have normally practised it, as
any help for faith in the future? Might it as well be abandoned, by
closing down the parish churches and getting together in the sitting
rooms? That's utterly unrealistic to me, and worse than that, it's
unjust to our tradition and the many people for whom the more
anonymous Mass is a genuine road to God.

Martha:
We're not quite saying that, Peter. I accept that the Sunday tradi-

tion is wise and rich and central, but I worry about the Sunday experience as it is found by many of the younger generation. Of course we would retain the big church, but it will need to alter its wavelength, to recognise that the culture of obedience is now a minority phenomenon. It will need to learn a new language of celebration, of witness, of preaching, of prayer. It will need the courage to escape the trap of being rushed, as you say. What's wrong with taking one's time a bit more? We're saying that the Sunday is central, but that it won't serve the faith needs of the future if it is carried in the same way as in the past. It could even become a source of unbelief to continue in the old mould.

Paul:
I think I sympathise more with Peter than he realises. Take your last remark, Peter, about Mass being a genuine road to God for many people. If that is true, then I have no complaints to make. But I fear it is increasingly untrue, and I go along with Martha in her sense of a great divide between generations as to what gives them spiritual nourishment. I'm beginning to see that the big-church experience of Mass seldom gives the kind of nourishment that is needed for faith today. It did in the past, but that was a very different world. I'm interested in people having any opportunity to meet Jesus Christ. If Mass is not serving that central necessity of evangelisation, then I have two questions: can it do so if properly re-directed? or if it cannot do so, where else can we look for places or times where faith can be fostered? And I think I know the answers to my questions, at least in general terms. With Peter I see the Sunday Mass as a potentially rich place of conversion for those who are reached by that occasion (and this would include substantial numbers of the younger generation as well). But for those who will not be reached by this vehicle of faith, we need other means. There are those who are present but who remain psychologically unreachable. And there are those who are absent but who are far from being convinced atheists. For both kinds of people the need is the same: how do we move from a largely church-based and inherited religion to a more personal and Christ-rooted faith, one that will bear fruit in a very different society from the past.

Martha:
But how do you even begin to enter into worthwhile contact with those who stay out of contact with the Church?

Paul:
In fact the Church has quite a range of other contact points for those who are more distant. I'm thinking especially of some of the key moments of life like marriage, of baptism of a child, or times of bereavement. The contact here can be merely nominal, or with a bit of imagination, it could be very fruitful. And these moments are often the only real opportunities for evangelisation with people who either do not practise, or for whom practice has degenerated into an empty duty unopen to change.

Peter:
Grateful as I am for Paul's defence, I find myself again in the position of saying—that's unrealistic. How can a busy priest have that kind of time for every couple who come to arrange a baptism, and who may be non-practising? The most he can do is be pleasant, and, perhaps, encouraging to them, but limited by time to a very short meeting.

Paul:
That's what I would mean by needing imagination. You don't have to think of priests as doing everything. For some of this gentle work of evangelisation of the lapsed, a fellow lay person could be much better. It would require some training and some teamwork, but it's not beyond the bounds of possibility to have a small team of suitable and committed people in every parish who would be able to sit down with the lapsed on these occasions and discuss the situation. A less clerical Church is part of my vision.

Martha:
I'd go further along that line; sometimes I don't think priests are going to be that important at all. It's in the home that future is lost or won for faith. And when I listen to my older children, I'm surprised they believe at all. They've inherited "an unhappy religion", as one of them put it to me, and when I'm really listening, I gather that some of that lack of happiness has been picked up from me as mother, and older people in general. My generation were very uptight about religion. If we're honest, we have to admit that most of it was a negative matter of avoidance of sin, or doing one's duty. There could be something deep too, but the dominant mood was

one of worry about doing wrong rather than being free. We lived totally under the shadow of the older kind of Church, and of religion, as obedience to authority. Looking back now it was a secure world, but one doomed to collapse. I think it was built on the sands of fear rather than on the rock of personal faith. And we're all marked by the struggles of making that transition. But for my children, anyway, the centre of gravity has changed entirely. They have little fear at all, and even if they had it doesn't seem to influence them much.

James:
In us, that fear gave birth to a religion that still remains too inward-looking. Not only did faith get reduced to religious duties, it also became divorced from being a way of courageous living. The main message that came across was strong ad restrictive: play our church games according to the rules. We never heard, with any per-suasiveness, that to be a follower of Christ means trying to con-front the established values of the world. The Bible often spoke of idolatry, the falling for false gods. I think we're surrounded by systematic idolatry. And we would be far too innocent if we failed to see that. The driving seat of our society is occupied by a system of values that is quietly subversive of Christianity: success, com-petition, the business ethic, economics-as-salvation, and a powerful propaganda machine of glamour and gloss. If that is true, it's ridiculous to think that all religion needs is a little bit of renewal. It needs to go on the offensive—not in a tone of moan but of active prophecy.

Paul:
Again I return to my theme: being a follower of Christ means first of all knowing whom I'm following. It needs a conversion of heart before these fruits or actions that James is talking about can flow from faith.

James:
I'm dubious about conversion-of-heart evangelism, I'm afraid. Of course it can do good for some people, at least in the short term. But I see a danger of a very privatised vocabulary of religion being offered today, and one that fails to open its eyes to the social revo-

lution taking place. Too often I've seen a cosy Christ being offered, a Christ of self-acceptance, that robs the gospel of its demands. Go back to the gospel itself: certainly Jesus first attracted his disciples to "come and see", but he soon challenged them with a lot of bigger horizons: "unless you become a child...unless you take up the cross...love one another as I have...as often as you did it to anyone you did it to me..." The merely inner conversion is not Christian: "faith without works is dead".

Peter:
I feel we're wandering too far from pastoral reality. Our question is how faith can be fostered in today's situation, and I still hold that the Church is the one realistic foundation for most people. I accept that institutions are in trouble everywhere, that they are almost bound to fall behind the needs of the times. I accept too that much of what passed for religion in the past may have contained a fair deal of fear, even of superstition. I admit that the official Church seemed insensitive to many things—to the problems of injustice or sexuality, or the status of women. But however much one beats one's breast about church inadequacies in the past, the Church remains the only starting point for faith for most ordinary people.

Martha:
But which Church? May I put it this way: You men have a great ability for not starting from experience. I'm totally convinced that the future of faith will be decided by how people experience religion, as presented to them through churches, or in any other way. It will not be decided by theology, or catechetics, or small groups as such. It will depend largely on how ordinary but confused people can experience hope and love together. To make it much more concrete, I think a priest is wasting his time preparing a profound sermon if the mood of the church building on Sunday morning is all wrong.

Peter:
That's hardly concrete, Martha. How do you alter moods of buildings?

Martha:
You set out deliberately to change the relationship of priest and people to something less of teacher/children and more of—it's not

easy to label it—a mixture of leadership and friendship before God.

Peter:
I'm glad I pushed you; you've just come out with a pretty good definition of what the Church is trying to be.

Paul:
Except that I want to repeat Martha's question: which Church? I love the Church in all its complexity, its wisdom and its warts. But I fear that there is a blindness in church circles to the extent of the faith crisis. The things Peter either worries about or rejoices over, are just different from the things I want to give my energies to. Forgive me, Peter, if I oversimplify your position, but you tend to be preoccupied with quantities of measurable religion and with the numbers of those "attending the sacraments". Even that phrase belongs to another world than mine. Practice was a useful measuring rod in an older culture. Its decline is saying something important; what I hear it saying is that basic faith in Christ is absent or empty, or at least shallow. So I don't really want to talk about keeping up high levels of practice. That's only an expression of faith. We're back to a frequent debating point of these last years: has populist Catholicism in various parts of the world fallen into the trap of being over-sacramentalised and under-evangelised? Is the Church still thinking of faith as nourished almost exclusively by sacraments? Could it be that there is another and missing factor? Sacraments nourish faith for those who have it first. They are no longer genuinely serving the faith needs of the younger generation who may not have the same roots in faith at all. In the long term it's pastorally pointless to insist on an "obligation to attend Mass" if the experience (as Martha highlights) seems more like a penance or if no previous personal sense of Christ has been reached.

James:
I think I see a different missing factor. It seems that each of us could be stressing quite different missing factors. Peter worries about what is lost when people leave the traditional practice of religion. Martha puts a lot of emphasis on people and their experience, and the world of everyday relationships as the place

where faith is either real or unreal. Paul sees the missing factor as some kind of adult conversion to Christ, something all the more necessary because of the new social pressures. But my missing factor is different again. I have given up asking, "do I understand the meaning of the Mass?" in favour of, "what do I let the Mass do to me and through me?"; and more pointedly, I evaluate religion in terms of whether it fuels or changes my social commitment in concrete ways towards the building of a different world.

Martha:
Why do I hesitate to agree with you? What you are saying is so obviously true, and yet my reaction is "yes but..." I fear perhaps that what James is stressing can become dangerously cut off from Paul's insistence on conversion and from Peter's sense of the "ordinary faithful". Most of all I fear a kind of social vehemence without compassion for the slowness of people's hearts to change. I suspect a sin of pride against the complexity of any human community at this point in history. I think my key lies in community.

James:
So does mine, but in a community of active service and critique. Of course it must find its ultimate roots in personal faith, but it must not be a community of mutual support only.

Peter:
I would hope that I'm talking about community as well—the people of God, a unity with a huge variety, including many different levels of belonging.

Paul:
And I would still be stressing the more individual decision of faith. A decisionless faith will never survive the new world that Martha has pictured. A decisionless faith will only drift and never have any possibility of lasting commitment such as James is calling for. But of course that decision is something possible only with and within the community that is the Church.

Peter:
We seem to have reached a certain convergence from our

divergences, and I have a final insight to offer. Perhaps the Church is a community of communities. It has both bigness and smallness. It needs both. Our tensions are in fact healthy—a bit like that diversity of ministries praised by St Paul in Romans 12. Unity need never mean uniformity.

So to return to my questions at the beginning—which view of the future do we hold, the view of majority church belonging or majority lapsing? The simple answer is that we cannot know and so we have to work on both possibilities. That does not make things nice and clear, but I think it makes our diversity not only healthy but essential. And perhaps that is a good note to end with.

10

A DEVILISH EXHORTATION CONCERNING CLERGY

This fantasy has been inspired by the celebrated Screwtape Letters of C.S. Lewis. It presumes that the task of undermining the faith in Ireland has been given to a team of demons and that within this team a sub-committee is charged with the business of looking after the clergy. A speech delivered to this task-force is reproduced here. The speaker is a senior and experienced tutor in temptation.

Gentlemen of the fire, you are a chosen band, singled out by our high command for a uniquely important assignment. It is one that our leader has committed to you because he views it as essential for the general kidnap of young people. You therefore are the hoof-picked ones, destined to bring about this goal. Your purpose is simple—it is to side-track any pastoral efforts by the clergy to adapt to the new world that has engulfed them and their Church these last years.

As your research will have already shown you, priests have entered a danger zone for the future of faith. This has been happening through out best endeavours for nearly a generation, but unfortunately they have recently begun to wake up to this fact. A decade ago your task might have been easier because one could then rely on a certain blindness to the new situation. But time has altered these agents of the Enemy, and nowadays they can prove impervious to our usual opener—the strategy of forgetfulness. That method may still work with some and if it does, so much the better; if they can be made to ignore the crisis, we simply take their people by slow surprise. I repeat: *slow* surprise. Slowness is part of our secret strength and our main consolation in distress. Remember that we are interested in the long-term and that even in our fallen state we have retained the virtue of patience. Because it is the long-term killing of faith that concerns you, never be dismayed over the occasional short-term defeat. Needless to say, I regret the so-called renewal made possible by papal visits, missions, novenas, and groups of all sorts (prayer groups, youth groups, social groups, marriage groups—a tedious litany). Such groups are indeed dangerous to us if they lead people to new freedom where they can have contact with the Enemy together, but I console myself that the impact of these efforts seldom lasts for long. Without follow-through, they can in fact lead to a very useful sense of disappointment—useful because our best moment is always found when a person feels let down by everything and everybody: it is then stupidly easy to get them to feel let down by the Enemy (if he exists at all for them).

From the outset, then, let us be clear about our goals. They are long-term objectives within which your role is quite specific. To you is given the commando task of attacking the traditional leaders of faith, the priests. By working diligently on them, you must provide us with the cornerstone for building a pagan Ireland. In pointing out this great honour of your calling, I intend no discredit to our other brethren of the fire who have been doing trojan work in other areas. We salute especially the task-forces engaged in specialised work with families, or education, or economics, or youth. We pay particular tribute to the sub-committee on social change which has been at work for two decades now, and whose efforts are only now bearing fruit. They have prepared the way of confusion that we inherit as our principal weapon. And now to you falls the decisive challenge of building on that confusion to ensure the impotence of our well-intentioned clergy.

Oh they are well-intentioned, and, as I was saying, they are worried in a new way about their work for the Enemy. They have begun to realise that not all is well with the younger generation and they are scratching their heads about this. What are we to do with them at this point? There is always a danger that they could become worried in a fruitful way (fruitful for them and for the Enemy); but there is also the possibility that we can channel that very worry into something that would prove fruitful for us. Do not be offended if I offer you a brief "renewal course" (as they would say) in some of our basic principles. Take the example of someone who realises that they have "sinned": that realisation can be a dangerous truth from which they turn to the Enemy, or it can be merely a depressing insight into the futility of trying to improve at all. To encourage that second reaction has been one of our most successful ploys for as long as any of us can remember. Remember Eden. Our key victories have always been when we can keep a person stuck in a negative attitude. Our success in outer "falls" is merely preliminary to this deeper take-over. Apply that familiar principle to these priests in their present situation of confusion and anxiety. Work on their worries in order to keep them merely negative.

In practice how will you achieve this? Simply by the old trio that we are expert in inducing: Fear, Anger, Despair. Let me unwrap these for you. Fear: anyone will be afraid when their familiar world seems to crumble around them. Something of that kind is happening to your priests just now as they face the phenomenon of non-practice and a new generation that seems to be less interested in their churchy world. Right then, keep it churchy. Let their fears keep them locked within their older patterns of work and of relationships. This will lead the older men to abdicate the youth field (even though they could be excellent agents of the Enemy if their confidence held). All they would need is to let go of their church moulds and speak the truth of their faith honestly and personally. But our strategy is to play the service of the Enemy. As for the younger clergy, let their fear of failing the Enemy lead them into an activism without reflection so that they "burn out" in various ways, more of that later. For the moment it is enough to see that you build on fear in somewhat different ways with priest of different generations.

After fear or even panic, the next stage to encourage is any version of anger. Just as happiness is a most dangerous sign if any of the Enemy's ambassadors, a certain note of lament or condemnation of reality is perfect for our purposes. It works wonders with the younger lapsers when they find their faith-confusions compounded by the human unattractiveness of the Church and its frontline representatives. So get the priests stuck in a tone of hostility to life. Let me offer you a precious memory of my own: I recall with special pleasure my own success through a sermon at midnight Mass one Christmas. The church was full of those hangers-on who only turn up at Christmas and for whom it was imperative that they do not hear anything that might touch their lives or attract them back to the Enemy. I worked on my man, who had had a hard day in the confessional, and the result was that he devot-

ed his entire Christmas sermon to giving out about those who left it
so late to come to confession; then to my delight he launched into a
general denunciation of youth as having no proper sense of sin. It
was blissful—the happiest Christmas I ever had. And the lesson for
you is obvious: fuel that dull anger born of fear, and so keep them
"giving out" about behaviour and well away from sharing their so-
called Good News as something alive for them. There is nothing
more likely to "turn off" the younger generation than a religion of
fear preached in a tone of condemnation.

As to the third of my negatives—despair. Perhaps that word is
too dramatic. You won't have many suicides among the clergy, but
you can induce a lot of everyday hopelessness. When that mood is
dominant, they will give our plans little trouble. You have nothing
to fear if they become religious functionaries, staying entirely with
the converted minority. For our long-term plans that minority is
fairly irrelevant. Of course, it may be more complicated to induce
some form of despair among the more activist clergy. Later on I
shall explain the "judo" principle to you, but for the moment it is
enough to point out that isolation is a fertile breeding ground for
discouragement among the idealists. Isolation from one another
and from the Enemy. Isolation allows us to distort their reading of
reality, or insinuate that they are getting nowhere and that nobody
appreciates their efforts. If their activism is accompanied by losing
the taste for that treacherous occupation called personal prayer,
then you have won the day. Discouragement will arrive as fatigue
and frustration mount. Stealthily—do be patient—you will have
stunted the missionary dreams of the idealists and you will have
thwarted the Enemy, not by robbing Him of His tools entirely, but
simply by blunting them.

Of course at any of these three negatives phases, you should
never neglect the personal life of the priest. Try to ensure that his
insecurities over pastoral work are mirrored in some personal conflicts as well. Any of the hardy annuals will serve here: start with
externals such as possessions, drink, sex and so on, and then you
will be able to move on to a hardening of attitudes, to feelings of
self-resentment and uselessness. This routine manoeuvre may be
boring for you but it still has its part to play in the overall undermining of the fruitful servants of the Enemy. Old ways are best!
And talking of your own reactions to this task, you will certainly

have to endure disappointment and many boring hours on the beat. The objectives will never be attained as easily as my outline to you here might suggest. It will require considerable ingenuity on your part, but then a uniquely satisfying prize awaits you. Imagine the downfall of Ireland into something of the spiritual state of the once proudly "Catholic nations" of Europe. Keep this in mind and you will not lose heart on the long road ahead.

The more time I spend outlining all this to you, the more I am convinced of the utter simplicity of our Great Plan. So far it can all be summarised in two easy steps. Number one: if possible keep your men blind to the realities of the new environment; if that works, you have little to worry about, because the undermining of faith will take its course in its own time. Step two: in case they awaken to some of the complexities of the new world around them, then hit them with confusion, fear, anger, depression; if this succeeds, then you will have turned them inwards towards self-absorption and paralysis, when the enemy wanted them to foster what he calls generosity and mission.

But all that I have said so far represents only one essential part of your battle—getting your victims into various states of withdrawal or of desolation. You have two other major fronts to fight on and these I want to touch upon now. The first one concerns not so much their own inner attitudes as their understanding of the new world. And the second, closely linked to that, has to do with avoiding certain dangers to your whole mission.

How do your victims interpret the present? Your aim is to tempt them to understand this radically new situation with an old mentality. If this succeeds it will automatically block their way to any creative responses. Let me spell this out more precisely. Priests in many countries have been very much men-of-the-Church, in the sense that by serving church activities they have for generations served the faith of the vast majority of their people. It has been very frustrating for us as long as they had that unquestioned fidelity of a traditional society. They have been used to thinking of themselves as administering a sacramental system, and in the older society this has worked far too well for the Enemy. They have focused their preaching on the preservation of church practice. They have been accustomed to being obeyed and respected as representatives of the Church. My advice is beautifully simple:

keep them inside that older way of seeing their role. If you manage to imprison them within that way of thinking, they will never notice how out of tune they are becoming with the needs of the majority.

You could accuse me of false optimism if I did not face the fact that this younger generation in Ireland remains ridiculously faithful to church-going. Of course it is on the decline. But it is still worryingly slow in its decline. I have pondered this at length and come to the conclusion that we have nothing to fear provided this custom remains on the level of external behaviour. Even if people are annoyingly slow to let go of this tradition, it need prove no lasting blockage to our plans unless, my comrades, one of my deepest fears were to be realised. The greatest and most tangible danger to your mission is that the priests of Ireland might shift their priorities to evangelisation, and that they might use the Sunday contact as a gateway to that explosive area. What would that mean for us! I speak these words to you with "fear and trembling" (to cite from one of the Enemy textbooks). It would mean that people might begin to have a personal sense of relationship with out Arch-Enemy, Jesus Christ. If that were to happen our entire venture would fall asunder. It would mean that the sacraments would again become "meaningful", as they say in that younger generation. It would mean that the Church, instead of being seen as merely an institution, might be experienced as a community of believers and disciples. It could even lead to a widespread outbreak of prayer. And worse still, there would be the distinct possibility of a big-four alliance between faith, community, prayer, and action-for-a-different-society. You are right, dear comrades, to shudder at that four-fold apocalyptic vision—because our whole strategy is the opposite of those four. We work for shallow faith where we cannot achieve non-faith. We strive for an off-putting and authoritarian Church that seems interested only in hollow conventions (*seems* is enough—appearance is all). If there is any contagion of prayer, we try to keep it either a very "spiritual" leisure activity cut off from life or else humdrum and unfruitful, never the source of growth in that perverse trinity of faith-hope-love. But if Christian believers were to become committed to "transforming their society" as their jargon has it, and if this were genuinely rooted in faith and not in fear-anger-depression, then, brethren, we would be in deep trouble. All the magnificent efforts of our sub-committee on social change

have been aimed at creating a society of drifters, lured by the surface life. Thus any decision to shape a different type of society
would be fatal to our plots—if it succeeded. But console
yourselves—that is a huge IF.

Returning to our special field of the clergy, let me reiterate,
like all good pedagogues, the key points of my discourse thus far.
Keep them worried. Keep them hankering after the old ways. Keep
them from falling into this fashion for evangelisation. That document from Rome in 1975 could prove most difficult for us, except
that we exploit their healthy scepticism for documents. The same
applies to their own local letter on justice a few years ago. You need
never be too upset when your men begin to discuss these things, or
when they read books or articles, or sit at lectures. The danger
point for us comes only when the new insights are heard as a call
from the Enemy for action. Indeed until that point arrives, it can be
a very fruitful exercise to let the men flirt with their new ideas. It
can heap coals on the fires of their vague uneasiness and then it can
become one more weapon in your war of attrition, the old faithful
of false hopes. This is particularly applicable to those of you working in seminaries or in smaller religious communities.

By the way, our special secretariat has produced a short but excellent handout on enemy methods of evangelisation which will be
available to you after this session (and which is printed at the end of
this text).

Already I have hinted at one of the principal dangers you
might face, the off-chance that the priests would opt to be missionary in a new way. However, I must alert you to various con-
tingencies that might arise, so as to prepare you to counteract them
with suitable infernal skill. (In this respect the leaflet from High
Command entitled *Deflecting the Priorities* should be meditated
daily by all of you). Even now I discern pockets of resistance to our
undermining process. I am not referring to those naive forms of
trying to stem the tide of social change: they are weakened from
within by being grounded in panic or negativism. I have in mind the
potentially serious attempts by your clergy to develop new scaffolding, new supports for belonging to the Enemy. Here another of
our ancient arts may well prove vital in any counter-offensive. The
art is "judo" and the goal is always excess and divisiveness. Let me
refresh your memory about "judo". In that art, if an opponent
comes against you, you do not push him away.

Instead you take the momentum of his attack, and with a little extra push you send him flying further than he meant in the direction he was moving. In short, he goes over your shoulder and falls on his face. The "judo" principle is the root of all heresy and schism. You use other people's energies to further your own designs. In practice this means your victim becoming so involved in something that he and his circle lose contact with the real world and with the all-too-real Church. You blind them to everything but their own little wavelength, and sooner or later they fall out with everyone else. This can apply to individuals or to communities; in fact it works particularly well for so-called experimental communities within religious congregations.

Alas, there will be cases where this form of "judo" may not suit, and therefore you will need an alternative plan to sap or divert the energies. I would strongly recommend playing on the sensitivities of the active and creative priest (especially in the singular). Inevitably he will run into some opposition or criticism or misunderstanding. All you need to do is exaggerate his feelings of not being appreciated so that he eventually undergoes a "judo" collapse—either through anger with others or else through a sense of futility within himself. To prepare for this work you would be well advised to study previous case histories in the recent records section of the High Command archives. There you will discover that the most frequently recurring factor in men leaving the ministry was a kind of workaholism in someone who experienced no real support from friends, no relevant guidance from any mentor, and little trust in his official superiors. Plenty for you to work on there.

Fellow fiends, as I draw to a close, a damnable apprehension has just seized me. I have outlined to you a comprehensive but top secret plan for the gradual neutralising of Enemy agents. But imagine if this conference dungeon had been bugged by the Enemy and if he were to let his agents know of our strategic assault plans. That could spell disaster. If they knew our ways, they could wage, under his guidance, a most efficient counter-offensive. And so if any of you are captured in Enemy terrritory you know what is required of you in terms of silence. On a more practical level, some of you, inspired with great zeal and diligence, have been tape-recording this exhortation of mine. Thank you for your interest.

But I must now insist, for security reasons, that you destroy the tapes before leaving Pandemonium on your Irish mission. *Heil Hell!*

HANDOUT
prepared by the Special Secretariat
for distribution at the Pandemonium meeting
of the ICSC
(International Clergy Sub-Committee)

Attention is drawn to the dangers of Enemy agents finding any strategy of evangelisation and to the particularly insidious practice, in some places, of having a plan for pastoral contacts. One such method involves four steps, and it is essential that all our agents should know of this counter-offensive.

Step one: This concentrates on images of the Enemy and on the fact that he has a plan for people's happiness. The basic idea is that we have sown false and fearful images of the Enemy (which is true) and that the first step must be to establish a picture of Him as loving father, as offering "fullness of life" and all those other phrases used by his Son.

Step two moves on to the realities that separate people from that plan. The aim is to awaken "a genuine sense of sin rooted in trust" rather than our favourite feeling of mere guilt rooted in self-blame. Successful Enemy agents have actually managed to bring people to great freedom at this point through their sacrament of Penance.

Step three introduces the Arch-Enemy and intruder. If people have realised anything of the love of step one, or of themselves as loved sinners in step two, then they can be dangerously ripe for a new "friendship and companionship with Jesus Christ" here in third place. This movement is often crowned through another sacrament—Communion.

Step four is the point where our defeat can be total because it aims at a change of governemnt, from us to them. It comes about when people understand that "faith in Jesus Christ calls them to live differently" and when they actually begin to choose according to another measure. The danger signal here is the vocabulary of conversion, or "Kingdom"—but only when it is actually lived.

11

TEN POINTERS FOR TEACHERS

This is a section of the book which I feel ill-equipped to write because I have had no training in catechetics, nor have I had to stand in a classroom and teach religion over any length of time. Nevertheless, it would be a sad omission if the school's role in faith-fostering were neglected in these pages. So I have opted for a brief set of "pointers", and I leave it to teachers themselves to judge their truth and applicability in the classroom world. These statements have come home to me from talking to teachers and, also, from my own experience of dealing with the past pupils of secondary education when they come to university. Any one pointer taken on its own might seem a bit unbalanced, but together the whole set is meant to evoke the complexity of the challenge posed to the teacher of religion by the relatively new secular culture of their students.

1) Broaden the agenda

It is one of the golden rules of any counselling not to take the problem as first presented to be the full picture. And so too with faith. The rather argumentative and hostile tone adopted by many teenagers over morality or church-practices may be only the tip of the iceberg of a deeper confusion. That confusion is not specifically religious, but extends to the whole question of the credibility of any traditional values today. The surface aggressivity or disinterest may, in fact, be a sign of a frustrated hunger for meaning, and ultimately for God. Therefore, the teacher has to be able to broaden the agenda in the sense of accepting the moods and taking the issues as posed; but he or she has to keep wider horizons in mind, and try to transpose the question into that bigger perspective. For instance, the question of church attendance cannot be allowed to occupy the whole field—its resolution requires some sense of faith in Christ. This very issue will be found explored in "letter to a church atheist" later in these pages.

2) The relationship is more important than the content
Of course the content of the religious curriculum is crucial (and
thesis nine will stress one aspect of it); but even more crucial is the
relationship between teacher and pupils. Insofar as we are talking
about the communication of personal faith and not just about the
clarification of doctrines, this emphasis becomes central as a starting point. The teacher of religion is more than simply a professional explaining something from a book or about a book. Instead,
he or she is asked to offer something different from the other sub-
jects. The element of witness is vital here, and the attitude to the
class will count for more than the perfect synthesis of theology.
Perhaps this can best be understood negatively: the content cannot
be heard until the relationship is right. Clearly this whole area
makes considerable personal demands on the teacher; it calls for
something of the conversion that Henri Nouwen (in *Reaching Out)*
described as the movement "from hostility to hospitality".

3) The school needs the home
The religious formation offered by the school is inevitably influenced
by the home-background, and so it depends greatly on whether the
home is co-operative or non-co-operative. And a home can be saying all the right things, but the stronger non-verbal message is that
faith is not too vital for the real concerns of life. It needs to be
recognised that the school is a relatively secondary influence in the
religious search of young people. In terms of contact hours, this is
obvious (and in terms of such measurement the school may be more
central than the parish). More positively, any effort by the school
to aid parents in their growth in faith will prove of immense help to
the fruitfulness of the religious education of their children. Indeed,
would it be possible for religious schools to make a contract with
parents that they will take an active part in the school's struggle to
build a world of credible faith for their children to experience?

4) The school can create a small community of faith
If the school sees its Christian mission in wider terms than the
teaching of doctrine to pupils, and if it reaches out to the bigger circle of families, then it can have many of the advantages of the small
community of teachers, students, and parents. We need units
smaller than the parish, and yet bigger than the home. The self-

understanding of the school can be called into new fields by this development. Even within its own day-to-day operations the school can cultivate the community dimension (rather than the management model) by trying to build an atmosphere of freedom and human sensitivity within its own world. On this basis it could then move to becoming more a community of explicit faith, something all the more needed in a context of unbelief.

5) Faith goes through periods of development and periods of unripeness

This is at least partly inspired by the work of James Fowler on stages of faith. Certainly a sense of the development character of individual faith will help a teacher to realism over limitations, and, at the same time, to hope over future possibilities as yet unripe. Fowler would hold that teenagers cannot be expected to have reached the stage of faith-as-commitment. They will inevitably be struggling with a totally different agenda of their own emergence from childhood, involving their own self-discovery and quest for values. If Fowler is correct, the key development that can be expected in the mid-teens is that they grow in some sense of a personal relationship with Christ, but they will not emerge from convention into conviction during the years of their second-level schooling. This transition from inheritance to ownership of their faith is not usually possible until the early twenties. A corollary to this thesis could be that some explicit attention to developmental psychology could be a source of help to the senior students themselves. It could give them a bird's eye view of where they are now in their life's journey, and it could give them confidence about future religious potentials as yet unready for blossoming.

6) Face the pressures towards unbelief

Because an increasingly secular context has created a different climate for growing up than was present a generation ago, the teacher of religion will need to offer his or her students some explicit understanding of these new influences, and to do so descriptively, honestly, and without hostility. This would entail at least four areas for special attention at senior level: social change and its impact on religion; psychological roots of alienation from faith; some outline of the classical positions of atheism in various forms;

clarification of the nature of faith itself in this context—as decision and involving darkness.

7) "Unless you become as a child..."

This is a version of the saying that faith is "caught" not taught. Beliefs *(fides quae)* can be taught, but the decision to say yes to God *(fides qua)* cannot be programmed. However much religious knowledge is assimilated on the level of understanding, it need never add up to faith on the level of personal commitment. There are many knotty questions here about the borderline between catechesis and evangelisation, and the role of the teacher of religion on that border. But what seems clear in the present cultural context is that preparing the dispositions of possible faith is a vital prerequisite to any communication of the meaning of faith. Thus, the teacher of religion has to find ways of awakening the capacity for wonderment (the "child") in each individual or in the group, and this can be done, not by talking about it, but by exercises to evoke the deeper hungers of each person. In this respect recent decades have witnessed much emphasis on pre-evangelisation, on the use of story and parable, and on the whole experiential component in religious education. Genuine awakening is more likely to take place through self-involving exercise (as in Brid Greville's work book on *The Mystery of God)* than through passive learning of some formula.

8) "Teach us to pray"

As part of this effort to educate through experience and through human depth, a particular place has to be given to helping young people to learn ways of personal prayer. In this respect it is worth recalling a secular definition of prayer from the poet W.H. Auden:

> To pray is to pay attention to something or someone other than oneself. Whenever a man so concentrates his attention—on a landscape, a poem, a geometrical problem, an idol, or the True God—that he completely forgets his own ego and desires, he is praying... The primary task of the schoolteacher is to teach children, in a secular context, the technique of prayer.

Some of the skills of stillness that have been popularised in recent years from a largely eastern spirituality, can prove attractive even in a classroom situation. All the teacher needs is the confidence to guide the group into simple methods of finding inner quiet. These arts of silence-making do not constitute prayer (no more than catechesis equals faith), but they can help greatly to bring students to deeper thresholds of freedom within themselves and, hence, to the possibility of a fuller listening to the Scripture as God's word to them. From this deeper and quieter encounter a more mature form of prayer can be born, and this can be the essential springboard for entry into other forms of more communal and liturgical worship.

9) "Be ready to give reasons for your hope" (I Peter 3.15)

Just as doctrines without experiential roots will remain conceptual and unreal, so too, experiences without understanding will fade. Bernadette MacMahon's report on teenagers, cited earlier in this book, showed that there was a danger of immaturity in faith on the knowledge level; for instance, the level of understanding both of God and of the Eucharist shown by more than half of the seventeen-year olds was judged to be weak or unacceptable.

In Ireland, in recent years, there has been considerable debate about the introduction of religion as an examination subject for the Leaving Certificate. On balance I would vote in favour of this as a way of giving intellectual backbone to the religious classroom. More important still is the need for some imaginative apologetics—not necesarily one that claims to 'prove' the existence of God but one that offers a set of signposts and stories for intelligent wonder. Such a new apologetics should begin not with questions of 'objective' truth but with issues of self-freedom. How can I recognise where I am unfree for faith? Where do social pressures reduce my religious potentials? A second stage might evoke some of the great journeys towards the discovery of God—such as the contrasting conversion stories of Augustine or Newman. A third stage would mean crossing the threshold into *the* source of faith, which is the love story of Revelation.

10) "There you see it: faith and deeds working together" (James 2.22)

Christianity is more a way of living than a way of understanding life, and so the full horizon of religious formation must include a challenge on this level of life-choices. This emphasis on action has been explored by Thomas Groome in his book *Christian Religious Education,* and I would not be capable of adding to what is richly argued there. From the point of view of this book, it is useful to insist that the deepest denial of God is a refusal of love, and that in the light of the Last Judgement parable of Matthew, chapter 25, the simple truth is that active love is more important than explicit faith. The ideal of Christian education is not ethics but a committed life with Christ; a faith alive in action. For many of the more socially alert young people it is faith-minus-justice that has become incredible. Any reduction of faith into pietism is sensed by them to be unworthy of their serious attention. St. James might say "and rightly so".

Conclusion:
In no way does this set of suggestions intend to cover all the aspects of the teaching of religion. If there has been no mention of sacraments, that is because this topic has been touched on elsewhere in the book. If there is nothing directly about Scripture or about moral education, that is because the angle from which these headings came was the challenge of unbelief today. Against this background, the first five pointers focus on the pre-conditions for the communication of faith in education at present. They point to the wisdom of seeing the whole picture: not just school on its own, but family contexts as well; not just the often blocked phase of adolescence, but progress towards adult decision; not the restricted field of complaint against church-religion, but real issues of faith in Christ. In this light, the remaining five headings move into some of the areas central in any religious education today. These five pointers outline a certain progression: from acknowledging the problems of our culture to awakening genuine religious hunger; from this openness of disposition to the personal listening that is prayer; then from this experience of the language of personal faith to a more intelligent grasp of the meaning of faith today; and finally from understanding the faith of the Church to the challenge of living it in a world of such hedonism and inequality. To stress any one dimension at the expense of the others would be a distortion.

It would seem that the crucial bridge to be built in religious education today is one that links human experience and faith-listening. Human experience ("from below") was the focus of the first six pointers; faith-listening ("from above") is at the heart of the remaining four. It is only too easy to succeed in one area and still leave the bridge unbuilt. Various sects seem to fall into this short-term procedure: the Eastern types offer an intense but divorced spiritual experience, whereas the more fundamentalist Christian groupings base themselves on a mindlessly literal listening to Scripture. The real challenge to the catechist is to move creatively back and forth between the richness of experience and the different levels of faith-listening—prayerful, intelligent, active. It is one thing to offer some limited but ideal schema here in print. It is quite different to seek an integration of these pointers in the everyday of the classroom. But at least they might serve as a reality-check to discern and evaluate what is actually happening.

12

A LETTER TO PARENTS

Dear Parents,

You tell me that some of your older children "seldom go to Mass any more". You ask what are you to think and, more anxiously, what are you to do? I don't know that I have any neat answers but, perhaps, I can offer some perspectives.

First of all, I don't want to say, "Shrug it off and forget it". It can be serious when one of your teenagers drops religious practice, especially when it lasts for years. But, I wonder what is it really expressing? My words to you will be trying to approach the issue from different angles. It's not a complete answer but rather a set of suggestions which I hope may help you not to panic too much.

Non-practice can often be just a reaction against the accepted way of life. As you know, some such reaction is inevitable as part of the rough process of growing up. A painful moment in the youthful journey towards finding oneself can involve rejecting what is cherished by one's parents. It's part of a shaky insistence that one can stand on one's own feet—an insistence that is often noisy because it is insecure.

When I was fifteen, I suddenly began to despise the kind of music my father loved (and which I, too, loved as a child). I chose my own kind of music which he could not stomach at all. Looking back now, I can see what neither of us could see clearly at the time, namely, that the tension was not about music but about me—or rather about us. My father tended to be hurt that I had rejected his taste. And, yet, adolescence meant that I had to find exits from his expectations. I had to separate myself from the little boy I used to be. And separations are often painful. Later, of course, I came back to allowing his music a place in my own horizon. But I had to find that horizon first. So my first answer to you is that some kicking over of parental traces is part of growing up. It need not always be dramatic or even hostile. But it is good to recognise it as a stage on the road to identity and maturity.

At this point I can hear you objecting, "We had our difficulties in our time and we didn't stop going to Mass—we didn't
even think of not going to Mass. Why is it so different now?" I like
quoting the answer given by a student: "You were never my
age"—meaning that we were never eighteen in 1986. So, as well as
the age-old conflicts of growing up, we have to allow for the particular pressures of this generation. And here I want to stress that
confusion about religion is only part of a more general confusion in
being young at this time. It's a cliché, but none the less true: this is
an age of transition. The very air we breathe, so to speak, is full of
new elements not present in the fifties. It's easy to list the big words
that sum up our changes: urbanisation, affluence, education,
media, travel, pluralism, pop culture, permissiveness. What they
add up to is the fact that we all move in a world vastly different
from when you yourselves were growing up.

It is worth insisting that these new changes are not evil in
themselves. There is little point in moaning about the environemnt
or in thinking that the clock can be turned back to the safer world
of the fifties. The theologian Karl Rahner has put it like this: it is
not faith that has changed. What has disappeared is a whole cluster
of pre-conditions for the special faith found in a traditional society.
So we have today to move from convention (which you accepted) to
conviction (which we must now find). And the crisis of non-
practice has to be understood in this new context.

Because those of us born before 1950 grew up in a different
world of assumptions, it is easy for us to misread the level on which
teenagers are today speaking about religion and about Mass-going
in particular. Where you as parents quite naturally speak a
language of doctrine ("Mass means uniting yourself to Christ") or
of obedience (the obligation to attend on Sunday), this is seldom
the level on which your older teenagers express themselves. They
are more likely to speak a language of experience ("I find it boring") or of relevance ("It does me no good"). And never the twain
shall meet. At least sometimes that is the case. Often it is this
unrecognised clash of horizons that makes family arguments about
going to Mass so futile.

When I find myself in conversation with young people on just
this issue, I have to resist my tendency to talk theology, to jump in
to explain the meaning of the Eucharist. Because, that is not really

their question. Take, for example, the frequent accusation that Mass is boring. Usually I simply agree with this as a statement of experience. But, I also throw some of the weight back on the young people themselves: what do they bring to the altar? It is a contradiction to expect Sunday Mass to be relevant and alive if the rest of life is one of practical atheism.

And there is another angle of objection to Sunday Mass sometimes voiced by young people. It is one that parents may find quite shocking: they accuse us of sham religion, in so far as we put too much weight on external practice which can be divorced from any impact on how we live. The Irish Bishops' Pastoral *Handing on the Faith in the Home* pulled no punches on this point: "Young people in their teens are very sensitive to the contradiction between the way adults go to church and pray and want young people to behave, and the way they live themselves. Nothing is said more often by teenagers than that they are 'turned off' religion by what they see as the 'hypocrisy' in the religion of many adults... They are impressed only by deeds. The biggest obstacle to Christian faith today is not intellectual doubt. It is, quite simply, the un-Christian life-style of so many of us who think we are good Christians." Once again the question broadens out from the narrow issue of church-going as something to be obeyed. The problem of non-practice cannot be answered today in terms of older ways of conformity. Indeed, the problem of non-practice is a product of an older conventionalism meeting with new confusions on many levels. So, even a new understanding of the meaning of the Mass is only a partial answer. The meaning has to be lived and seen to be lived.

What then can parents do? I don't believe in forcing young adults to go to Mass against their will. In line with *Handing on the Faith in the Home,* the emphasis has to be on communication rather than on conformity. Speaking directly to the parents of teenagers, that letter said: "Perhaps the most important thing of all is to have time, to make time, for talking with your children and for listening to them, at every stage of their growth." In other words, the lines of dialogue need to be kept open in as unargumentative a manner as possible. Parents should be ready for aggressive pronouncements that seem to reject faith lock-stock-and-barrel. How many teenagers, in a tantrum or mood, have told a parent that they hated them, or hated "this house", or something to that effect? And you wisely wait without fully believing the words.

I've often heard from parents that the main obstacle is not angry words but the wall of silence that descends in mid-teens. Again, that may be inevitable as a phase of growth. It's a painful period, of course, for the parents themselves. Perhaps it is some help to recognise that something like this is bound to happen. Some teenagers "go silent", others "go deaf", in the sense of getting locked up in their own world for a time. This period asks of parents a delicate change in their role: from obedience supported by disapproval or approval to a new relationship of adult to quasi-adult.

How can you deal with this possible silence or deafness? Not by resentment, but by communicating acceptance and understanding. Even without saying it. You cannot *not* communicate, whether by words or by silence. It's far from easy to tread the tightrope between keeping supportive communications open and yet allowing freedom and privacy to the emerging adult. Once again, I am trying to situate possible trouble over religious practice within a larger context—within a difficult transition for both parents and teenagers. Stay in gentle contact as far as possible—allowing for the painful fact that a parent may, at times, be the last person able to help one of their own children. Remember this phase of growth demands, precisely, that the young distance themselves from parental influence. Above all, avoid having rows over religion. Pray for your daughter or son and pray for new wisdom for yourselves; keep the channels open; and wait, hoping that your own faith as lived through love will be seen now, even in silence. And appreciated later once the dark days pass.

The fact of running into some difficulties like this is not necessarily unhealthy. In our new environment, mature faith will no longer happen without some struggle. A challenge is both a moment of potential danger and a moment of potential growth. Without any doubt some young people today will go astray and will remain in a long-term confusion over Church and faith. For others a period of uncertainty and of groping may be of short duration, and may, indeed, be a purifying crisis on the road to maturity of faith and its commitments. Certainly the role of parents can be crucial at this time; a calm and gentle reaction to difficulties can make all the difference.

Our model here can be the Lord himself (in John's gospel, Chapter Four) dealing with a very wounded and confused woman at the well. She at first refused him a drink of water. She reduced his promise of living water to a question of buckets. She tried to argue about where one should pray or worship. She avoided her own real feelings of guilt and hurt. Jesus went along with her, very slowly. He "stayed with her", not angered by her aggressiveness or her changes of mood. He was waiting patiently for a moment of truth much more time than the few minutes required to read it. It is actually a conversation over a long journey towards finding God in spite of obstacles. In the light of this gospel story, we see it as part of the calling of Catholic parents today that they become, in new ways, wise companions to their children, as those children take their own difficult but exciting road to maturity and fulfilment.

13

LETTER TO AN IN-BETWEEN

From a religious point of view I see the younger generation as falling into three fairly different groupings. For one group (and I'm not going to guess at percentages) the bottom has fallen out of whatever faith and practice they may have inherited, and the result is that within the space of a few years the whole world of religion has come to mean very little to them. I sometimes think of them as victims of a kind of cultural injustice, meaning that the newer life-styles have robbed them of their roots and kidnapped their consciousness in different directions. The supports offered by Church-family-school have often proved inadequate to help them find any genuine faith for today. Of course this decline in faith can come in many shapes and sizes, some more conscious than others. I can think of some socially alert people who can be very angry with the Church and with religion, or else of others who seem to choose a greedy and selfish existence. But for the most part I would think of this first group as *departed victims,* let down by the fact that the older Church language rings hollow in their new world of experience.

Another group at the opposite end of the spectrum would include those fortunate ones who have managed to discover some new forum for their growth in faith. Very often they do this through belonging to some little community of people who are working—of course with struggles—towards some level of Christian commitment. Let me call these, deliberately echoing the Gospel, the *seekers-and-finders.* Here I'm thinking particularly of the huge burgeoning of Christian communities of mutual support and mutual challenge. Their diversity is like that so strongly encouraged by St Paul *(I Corinthians 12* or *Romans 12),* a diversity to meet various spiritualities and temperaments. Their unity, today, is that they all stem from the big Church, but sense the need for smaller unities within that larger tradition.

But for this occasion I want to focus on another middle group, whom I'll call the *in-betweens,* and who might well be more numerous than the two just described. These are young adults who continue to "practise", perhaps with less regularity than their parents would hope, but they have not opted out of the Church. Neither have they opted into any real Christian commitment. They remain in an undernourished limbo. They hang on to what their parents hung on to, but they are not their parents, and so what gave nourishment and support to their parent's faith can fail to feed their younger lives. They have inherited a rich convention, but they seldom experience its richness; instead they hold to the outer convention and lack inner conviction. A key question is how they might make that move from convention to conviction. This letter is one answer to one person in this situation. It is based on a real person, a young worker in electronics, but it changes some of the details of his situation in order to be helpful to a wider audience.

Dear D.,

Do you remember what you wrote months ago now? I've kept it as a marvellous image of your searching and your uncertainty, and I quote it back to you now at the beginning of this letter where I want to explore your religious position in public so to speak, because I'm sure that it will find echoes in many others in their early twenties. This is what you said about your own attitudes:

> I find the Church does not have a challenge for me. Maybe I have not found it. Who knows! I have a lot of doubts. While one may be a good Christian, a good Christian does not necessarily make a good Catholic. I therefore turn elsewhere for a challenge. Caving offers a greater challenge, as one is hundreds of feet below ground. If your light fails, one is lost and does not know which way to turn. Turn the wrong way, and one falls hundreds of feet, possibly to death. This where I stand as regards the Catholic Church. My light has failed, but I am afraid to turn in any direction lest I fall.

It's because of that final image that I've treasured that paragraph ever since you wrote it. It seems to capture that sense of being in-between about religion—neither at home in the faith of your childhood, nor ready to throw it all over. I get a double message:

on the one hand you are genuinely looking for something worth-while and challenging; on the other hand your experience of church religion leaves you dissatisfied and disappointed. Let me broaden the issue for a moment, because I think it applies to much more than the area of religious faith. You are now into your early twenties. Very likely your own personal needs have changed over the last five or six years, and perhaps you have recognised the changes. You are now thinking of marriage in a way that would not have been relevant to you at all at eighteen. When you are a teenager life happens, or at least that's the way it seems. Older people might ask: "What are you going to do?", or parents might get worried and ask: "When he's going to settle down or make some decisions?" And there *was* a clash between their language and yours—at least then. You preferred a rhythm of exploration, letting things turn up, getting enthusiastic over someone or something for a time and then moving on.

Living with and for happenings was fine for a while. But there's a vital fork in the road, one most people come to in late teens or early twenties, and I feel that you have arrived there now. It's as if one road continues downhill and the other uphill. The downhill one is signposted, so to speak, "life happens", and the uphill one has the sign "life is chosen". My point is that after a cer-tain stage the important things in life simply do not happen; they have to be decided on and often with difficulty. It can happen that you fall in love; it doesn't just happen that you *stay* in love. Perhaps "luv" happens and that's great, but "love" is chosen, and that is greater. Indeed, I hear from people involved in marriage counselling that something similar is surfacing there in recent years. Many young people have a much greater regard for intimacy and companionship between man and woman than was explicit in an older generation, and that is certainly a good expansion. But they often seem to have less awareness of the value of perseverance through difficulties. So the expectation of instant relating under-mines the hopes for lasting relationship. Whatever is to last will have to be chosen on the uphill road.

In religious ways too you seem to be at that same fork in the road. Notice again what you said yourself: your membership of the Church continues but as an external habit while the real light has gone out for you. Can you see that the light will not happen to go on again? Something is missing and it will stay missing until you choose to fill the empty space somehow. What is missing? I would guess quite simply—a personal relationship with Christ, or at least a relationship that does justice to your maturity of experience now. Insofar as that is missing, it's no surprise that the religious fidelities inherited from your parents don't hold together for you. Because those inherited fidelities need not add up to faith any more. Possibly in your parents' youth they did so, when the supports of a whole way of life were stronger. But not for you: you have to choose faith against the tide. Sure, you could hang on to the inherited practices as you are trying to do, but that level will never bring the "light" you hope for. If you only hold on to the externals, they will become emptier with the years, even if glimmers of faith and prayerfulness continue from time to time. That is what is likely to happen for someone growing into the world you have to live in. The only alternative is to choose a different level of faith for yourself. This would mean moving from mere inheritance to ownership of what you have inherited. If you can cross that bridge into a chosen faith, then the inherited fidelities may find meaning again, because they can come alive as expressions of what is their only core, a personal commitment to Jesus Christ.

Ah, but how? Where to begin? You've heard it all before, and it rang true, but little ever happened. Exactly. I repeat (at the risk of boring you): nothing will happen until you make it. What investment are you willing to make? Of time and regular time at that. In some kind of searching that you don't abandon at the first difficulty or disappointment. Let me risk a little tangent to explain what I mean through my own experience.

It's a key part of my calling that I try to pray every day. By that I mean spending an hour, perhaps broken up, in some kind of search for God. That pattern is now part of my way of life. I would feel strange going to bed if I had not had some exposure to prayer that day. But it's something that doesn't just happen. Up to a point yes: I've got into the habit of finding a space each day. It's still up to me what I do with that space and so there's a daily struggle, a daily decision. For me, too, it's easy to remain on the level of inherited fidelities, to put in the time and in fact to waste the time. What makes the difference is my attitude each time. It's always a battle to get in touch with my hunger. The Magnificat puts it, "the hungry he fills with good things, the rich he sends empty away''. Utterly true. If I'm "rich" in the sense of being self-satisfied and superficial, I go around in circles talking to my own little consciousness, but never really reaching out to God; and I go away unrefreshed, empty, a bit self-angry. Being "filled with good things" can take many forms, but it means that in darkness or in light the heart is slowly expanded into freedom and love by God.

You have your parallels to that. I don't necessarily mean that you need the same pattern of prayer. But you need some prayer, like breathing, to live as a Christian. Have you found a prayer form to fit you? You too have to get in touch with your hunger and follow it, as you did in that image of caving. Just as I need my daily scaffolding to remember Reality, and without it I fall into a kind of unreality, so you will need some concrete steps towards a deepening of faith.

What can you do in practice? Take you pick of three battle fronts and begin small on one of them. Let me put it with my favourite alliteration: commit yourself to some search of head, or of hands, or of heart. By "head" I would mean some programme of getting a more adult grasp of the meaning of faith. And there are very many avenues to deepen your understanding of God. The Scriptures are special here; how well do you know them, personally and prayerfully? Perhaps the crucial point here is that so many people try to survive on childhood images of God and so they court immaturity of faith. You often hear of people suffering with a false view of God as avenger or boss or enemy; yes, and the opposite is also true for people of a different upbringing—that God is seen as an easy-going-pal, a vaguely cosy God who makes no demands on them. Go back to your own statement about a religion that has never challenged you.

If by "head" I mean any route to a fuller understanding of God, by "hands" I mean the whole area of self-giving social action on some regular basis. It's always better to do this with a group of people and to have the chance to reflect together on what you do in the light of Christ. By "heart" I would mean some daily effort at inner space for God, some attempt to learn to pray more personally. And in recent years there has been much talk about skills of stillness that can help here (for instance, the books of Anthony de Mello or Mark Link). To this stress on prayer I can hear you saying, "but I wouldn't know how to begin". Right, I'll offer you one simple way of beginning. Step one: find time and place for quiet. Step two: relax into some inner silence, patiently focusing yourself through becoming aware of your breathing for a few minutes. Step three: take a scene in the gospel of one of the meetings with Jesus, for instance, John chapter four, where he meets the woman of Samaria. Try to make it real for you, entering into it personally. Step four: pause whenever anything strikes you and quietly voice your hopes, or listen to the invitation of Christ, or just rest in inner quiet in his presence. "Ask and you shall receive". And remember that scene is a long journey for that woman from being blocked and perhaps embittered (refusing a drink of water, wounded by broken relationships); through facing the truth of her life, understood by him; and through doubts, questions, even arguments about the liturgy; towards a moment of recognition of Jesus and then being free to go to others in a new way. There is a whole summary of a long process there. For you it might mean ten minutes a day for weeks on end, patiently and fruitfully keeping your appointment, even through times that will seem total failure.

As you see I've taken one line on the whole business of being a non-mediocre young Christian today. I've taken your situation of being "in-between", hanging on to practice but missing out on any challenge, and feeling dissatisfied with your faith-as-lived. I've tried to say, bluntly, that merely keeping the convention will not guarantee you the "light" you want. Without some personal relationship with Christ, nothing will last for long in your religion. And you have to choose to make that happen in some way, through some gateway that suits you. You may be surprised that I haven't spoken about the Mass, which you find somewhat of an empty experience. Exactly. As long as you come to it passively expecting it to do something for you, you are still in the language of "happening". The Mass is in crisis for many of your friends insofar as it is the only "religious" thing they do, and so it lacks any reality from other areas of life. The Sunday celebration is meant to be the crown of a Christian life, lived elsewhere than in the church building. If Mass is the only time of the week when there is any kind of gesture towards God, it would be surprising if it were not often boring or hollow. Of course we priests have to take our part of the blame for some of the boredom: our side of the liturgy can be shoddy, unprayerful, unimaginative and so on. But I also imagine that when you complain of boredom at Mass, a fair bit of it is imported by you across the church porch. By this I mean that you can come with empty heart (little prayer), empty head (weak understanding of our faith), or empty hands (little to offer from the action of the week). I'm being deliberately severe to make a point here: don't expect the Church or Mass to meet your spiritual needs provided you simply turn up on Sunday. That's too passive by far. It doesn't even begin to meet your own deepest self, nor does it allow for the undermining pressures against faith in ordinary experience now. Either you choose to swim against the tide, or else unconsciously you opt to drift with it. And so I come back to the main theme of this letter. I am convinced that the only worthwhile faith for the future is one rooted in personal decision, and that finds support with like-minded others. That seemed to be the cry of your own little metaphor about caving, challenge, light. Over to you. Where would *you* choose to begin to answer your own hungers?

P.S.:
I forgot to comment on what you called "doubts". What are we to do with "doubts"? They could be both normal and healthy. Normal because of the nature of faith itself: it is strange kind of knowledge, an "incomplete knowledge" as Thomas Aquinas liked to say. Healthy because what you call "doubts" could well be questions that need answers; they could be signs of undernourished understanding.

But there is another kind of doubt that is more difficult. It is more a mood than a real question; it is more vague than definite. It is rooted in the flux of one's feelings rather than in unanswered difficulties of the mind. And this more subjective kind of doubting is harder to deal with because it often links up with your personal experiences of life. Some people seem incapable of believing any good news, including the Good News of being loved by God. Due to scars in their own life-stories, the Gospel seems too good to be true. As St Augustine once put it, "someone who has had experience of a bad doctor can be afraid to trust himself even to a good one".

Doubts of the mind can be met by some clearer grasp of the meaning of faith. But doubts of the mood call for some new attitude, for a different relationship to oneself, to others, and to

God. Of course my two types of doubt may not remain neatly distinct. Underlying some vague sense of the unreality of religion there can lurk some quite false images of God. But often it helps to recognise which family your "doubts" belong to: whether they are questions in need of answers, or else psychological states in need of some new expansion and freedom, you have to decide to seek out answers or else to seek out new experiences of yourself and of faith. I seem to have returned to my chorus of this letter. Doubts will happen. You have to choose what to do about them. But knowing them for what they are is half the battle.

14

LETTER TO A CHURCH-ATHEIST*

Dear T.,

We met on the train from Sligo. You were with someone who knew me and so we got talking and entered into that lengthy discussion on religion. It was a most enjoyable journey, so much so that I want to gather the strands of that conversation together here—for you and for others.

At first we were struck on one or two points. Almost like a conventional opening in chess, you started with the question of Mass-going. You were brought up with this at the centre of religion. And now at twenty-three you find it empty and you only go when it would cause family tensions if you didn't. You seemed surprised that I wasn't unduly shocked by that revelation; but I've known for a long time how that is true for many of your contemporaries. What would be more rare is the eagerness to explore the whole question, an eagerness which made you seize our opportunity on the train. It makes a big difference that you continue to be conscious of your dissatisfactions over religion, and that you face your hungers with a lot of honesty. Some of the remainder of this letter may seem hard on you; indeed I'll be saying that some of your notions of religion are not worthy of you, to say nothing of God. But I begin from a sense of gratitude to you for our two-hour dialogue: it helped me also to clarify things—as you'll see.

Let me remind you of some of the steps in our exchange. When I began to broaden the agenda of our conversation, saying that Mass-going can make little sense without a context of faith, you immediately jumped in to say that you couldn't accept transubstantiation. And I responded, even a little sharply, that you were reducing faith to doctrine, and that your rejection of religion seemed rooted

*I coined this term when preparing an article on the atheism of James Joyce, meaning that some unbelievers are stronger in their rejection of Church than of God.

in fairly narrow interpretations of it. Looking back now, it seems
to me that you thought of Catholicism in terms of three main areas:
practice (Mass-going), doctrine (transubstantiation) and morality
(sexual norms). Whereas you tend to restrict religion to those three
compartments, my immediate response was to open a larger
perspective to discuss those three issues. Mass-going, for instance,
is one community practice, but it depends on other practices if it is
to make sense: it needs at least some spirit of prayerfulness and
some spirit of sacrifice. More of that later. Again, transubstantiation is one important doctrine, but taken out of its faith context it
can hardly be appreciated; it rests on belief in God becoming man
in Jesus and then continuing his presence with us in this special
way. So it would be a case of cart-before-horse to take it divorced
from the gospel and from faith in Christ. As for the Christian
norms on sexual behaviour, they will usually clash with the com-
monsense of the world. But I would want to insist on two important points here, first, Christian morality is much larger than sexual
norms and involves a whole way of life and of struggling for justice
in this world; and secondly, after ten years of priesthood, spent
largely with your age-group, I'm convinced that the Christian way
in sexual matters is both profoundly wise, and yet often incredible
in today's culture for anyone who has no personal sense of Christ.

But let us go further than simply pointing out inadequacies in
your images of religion. You remember that at one stage in the
train I got out a bit of paper and constructed a diagram to suggest a
different horizon on faith. I called it a map of faith-maturity and it
went like this:

COMMUNITY

INTERIORITY   COMMITMENT

REVELATION

I intended this to broaden your terms of reference. Thus on the
question of Mass-going, I was arguing that it is only one expression
of the *community* dimension of faith. If you experience it as a piece
of boring obedience, and if you have little sense of belonging to a
community, then it's not surprising if that practice goes dead for
you. Under the heading of "community" I am thinking of the need
to have a relationship with other believers and searchers. And I

would situate the problem of Mass, as many of your contemporaries run into it, within this larger picture of not experiencing a believing community. But the other three dimensions are relevant to the questions of Mass-going also.

By "interiority" I mean the whole story of a person's inner life; it would include the pattern of searchings which can be found in a different way in everyone. For some people it will mean a journey into some kind of prayer; for others it will cover moments of special awareness scattered through life, perhaps to do with nature, or music, or the turning points of decisions. In its more explicitly religious form, I gather that you got stuck with the notion of "saying prayers" and never had much experience of personal prayer. You have your own inner life, but one that never linked up with the religion you inherited. If you could make that connection, you could approach Sunday Mass in a different spirit.

I'm more and more convinced that the third heading of "revelation" is going to be the pivotal one for faith in your generation. Indeed the whole diagram could be called a road to "revelation". The community of the Church exists only to allow people to hear God (which is revelation). To be ready to listen to God is also the very purpose of any inner life by Christians. Without "revelation" the whole enterprise of religion has no anchor, no roots. In particular for your generation, without some personal discovery of Jesus Christ, the whole business of Mass-going can appear a hollow custom from another age. But let's be careful about that word "revelation" because it's one of those religious terms that can trigger off a merely stock-response. Take any good and unexpected experience, even our own conversation on the train. You could imagine yourself saying, "that was a revelation". It wasn't so much the fact that we were exploring new ideas, but rather the experience of meeting one another at a certain level of trust and honesty. Perhaps the key to "revelation" is less in the content communicated than in the relationship established. If so, the core of Christian revelation is God showing us himself in Jesus, and the main result—to use that cold term—is not new knowledge so much as a new level of friendship. Like on the train. From that relationship with Christ new knowledge of God becomes possible. But it's an unusual kind of knowledge. In your technology world you're used to finding out the truth for yourself, and by yourself. But here

the relationship of friendship is the indispensable setting, and
without it the new knowledge of God cannot be discovered. Your
horizons on religion were pretty undernourished on this point—you
thought of the whole thing more in terms of a convention than of a
relationship. That's what I mean by something both unworthy of
you and unworthy of God.

Apply that to your point about transubstantiation. My fear is
that your experience of religion to date has given you bits of
knowledge of Christ who is the centre of any doctrine. Any talk
about transubstantiation needs to be rooted in understanding the
gift of Jesus at the Last Supper. What did he do and what did he
mean? Why did he give that bread and wine to his little circle that
night with those words? And what could that scene have to do with
us now? Transubstantiation is one answer to one of many questions. To bandy it about outside the context of the Last Supper,
and without a sense of man's questions about that Supper through
the ages, is to reduce revelation to formulas. But the merely doc-
trinal is never the fullness of faith. Without the relationship of
friendship—the heart of revelation—those theological words ring
hollow, like answers without questions.

And so to the last of those four pointers, the one called "commitment". In theory this is straightforward; in practice it is difficult to attain. Jesus talking to Nicodemus said that the "man who
does the truth comes into the light" and St Paul stated bluntly that
"faith without action is dead". So Christian faith can never be the
real thing if it remains "undone" or unlived. It is much more a way
of living than a theory about life. To take John again, if "we are
children of the truth, our love is not to be just words but something
real and active". Why mention all this to you? Because I don't
want to defend religion except in its fullness—what it should be,
and what it may not often be in actuality. Without this fourth
dimension of faith, religion becomes stunted into something soft
and even escapist. But if I recognise Jesus as Lord (revelation), I
am called to change my vision and my way of acting. We started off
arguing about Mass-going, but we have to wonder about Mass-
doing. Indeed the very word Mass means being-sent; we are intended to be sent into life to struggle to build a more loving world. Now
I'll admit that this is an ideal. But even if we fail, Christians are
people who are trying to live up to this four-fold richness.

So, in short, I would sum up our conversation by saying to you: get the issues right. If you want to be an unbeliever, be a proper unbeliever, someone who has faced the full picture of what Christian faith is, and not someone who became disgruntled with Church externals for teenage reasons. The other possiblity is that you could begin a return journey to faith, not the childhood faith you outgrew, but an adult faith that awaits you—a way of life, and not just an ideology; a personal relationship, and not just a set of duties; a freedom to be fuly human, and not a cramping of your humanity.

15

LETTER TO AN ATHEIST FRIEND

Dear A.E.,

It may surprise you to find yourself addressed towards the end of this book. Because it is not really your kind of book. And yet indirectly you had a hand in its being written. In quiet moments of putting it together—often with drudgery and pain—I've remembered you as a kind of touchstone. I recall in particular one occasion when we talked and reached thresholds of understanding of each other, well beyond any mere arguing about my faith or your atheism. I look back on that conversation as showing me the meaning of that word "dialogue"; literally it means the exchanged word, and we were two whose words became reverent before our differences. We experienced, for a privileged moment, the thin line dividing the experience of faith from the experience of atheism. We saw that in spite of different interpretations of the journey, we shared a common commitment to travel hon stly along roads whose significance we see differently. We recognised the darkness and fragility of our certitudes. We uncovered together the hope not to waste this life or the talents given. We acknowledged the dividedness of heart that makes steady love so difficult. In short, we shared the experience of lives struggling towards meaning and freedom, and we knew that what separated us was in a sense secondary. Over both my faith and your atheism there lies a cloud of unknowing—neither of us can prove to the other the realities we darkly yet deeply believe. And at the centre of both our visions lies a shared longing for more light.

When you began first to talk about your personal position as an atheist, it was not long before I realised that here was someone who had got beyond the more usual stance that I call Church-atheism and had arrived with pain at a kind of God-atheism. Certainly, as you looked back on your teenage years, you saw your rejection of religion as rooted in all kinds of emotional turmoil and of rebellion against institutions and authorities. But since then, your journey has been deeper and more calm. As you put it, if there is nothing beyond, then we are terribly alone. You voiced both your opennes to God and your inability to find him. Your atheism came across to me as something far from cheap, rooted in both agony and commitment: agony, because you have worried over this question for years, and commitment, because you are someone very far from drifting through life, someone faithful to the values that you see. And here I want to pay you the tribute of not arguing with you over the existence of God. Instead, I simply offer you two things: one, a recognition of your honesty and goodness that makes me happy to be your friend; and second, a sense of sharing with you in an uphill search for what we called "wisdom".

So at the end of this little volume, many of whose pages you might think naive, I wanted to reach out again and to ponder with you the possibility of wisdom now. In one way the question is quite simple: people blessed (or cursed) with the education we have received know too many things in a scattered way, and have too little of anchoredness to gather what we know into living unity. Yeats was prophetic in describing his stage of life as doomed to suffer dispersal and yet longing for "simplification through intensity". That's us all right. Are we then crippled by our culture? Is there no way to wisdom left? The medieval harmony will not come again. The collapse of that integration is fairly recent: it made sense until we entered the complexity of knowing too much about ourselves.

But I think I see a costly convergence of wisdom as still possible, not a synthesis of the older kind, but a more personal journey that can be undertaken in different ways by you and me. I think of myself, in a very ordinary image, as standing on a stage, waiting for light. And I picture wisdom as a convergence of at least three spotlights, shining down from different angles. When all three are on, there will be less shadows, and a key to wisdom lies in the convergence of the three, not in any one light alone.

It was the light of imagination and its creations that first brought us into contact with one another. This is a world of wisdom as embodied in literature or cinema today. It has been said many a time that literature has become the unofficial theology for our unbelieving century—in the sense that images can capture the contours of experience with a richness beyond our usual chatter. As Rosemary Haughton put it, both theology and poetry aim to confront mystery, which is something "beyond speech but not beyond imagination".

A century ago Matthew Arnold predicted a new role for works of imagination—that they would assume the burden of spirituality for an age of doubt. Just to take a sample of Nobel prize-winners: writers such as Hesse, Faulkner, Beckett, White, or Solzhenitsyn have all become cult figures in our age of frustrated religiousness. And I have often heard you claim that some of this great literature expresses human depths much more adequately than any Church or theology. I see a paradox here. This literature is probably the most starkly and explicitly agnostic of any era to date, and yet it is far from being anti-religious. Think of the career of Aldous Huxley, moving from cynical satire to the exploration of the mystical in mankind. As well as being indifferent to conventional religion, a major thrust in our literature has been towards rescuing the spiritual dimension in some form.

There is, then, this first light, the wisdom of images, one that assumes a uniquely important role in this century's making of meaning. And we have both found nourishment of spirit in those worlds of imagination. But we also sense something lacking. Other hungers haunt us. One light of wisdom is not enough.

Another light is that experienced by the inward self, the strange story unfolding within each of us. For my part I would now find it hard to go for long without the soaking in silence and solitude that marks my daily routine. What happens within this framework of prayer is unpredictable, sometimes utterly empty and struggling and sometimes gathered into gratitude. I have spoken to you more than once about my habit of prayer and you always seemed to understand from your different position. We can agree at least on the human values at stake here, because we both recognise the need for the deeper self to breathe fresh air. It's a version of Plato's claim that the unreflected life is not worth living, or of Pascal's saying that most of human trouble stems from not being able to sit still in one's room. In our time this inner journey is exceptionally difficult to sustain, and it is one of my fears for you that you might not find a way of self-listening, or of being true of the depths within you.

How can one avoid malnutrition and mediocrity of the self-journey here, where the very quality of personal life is at stake?

And I say this, not from some superior position, but precisely from the evasions and complacencies that I encounter within my own commitment of trying to pray. The crunch along this way of wisdom is to keep going beyond the barrier of usefulness or felt rewards. What do you do with darkness when you run into it at any length? Our culture and way of life can seem a conspiracy to keep us from these forbidden zones of silence and darkness.

Of course the inner journey must be different for me and for you, but its core is much the same: it involves a certain attitude of opennes, a quality of listening in depth, a capacity to wait with self-patience. I think you agree with me on the dangers today, that we become sucked into a culture of externality. Anything of real value in intellectual work or artistic creation or political commitment will need this costly wisdom that comes from within the self. So far so good: we understand one another to this point. But we part company when I go further and say that only from a disposition of openness can Revelation be received and then faith be born. Although you cannot take that step, I am asking you to recognise what is involved and to see where it fits into my story of our wisdoms. Religious faith can be described in many ways—as an assent to God's truth, as a commitment to Christ's way, as "the assurance of things hoped for and the conviction of things not seen". Here I would express it as a personal recognition of a Revelation of love. And if that recognition is to take place, it will often happen as the climax of this journey of interiority. It will not happen from objectivising intellect and its inquiries—at least not from that alone. It will not happen from perusing the scriptures and their claim to Revelation. It will happen only when heart and mind and spirit unite into a decision of receptiveness, and when that moment of reaching out is blessed by becoming prayer. We can share the road of interiority even if our ways of imagining our journey's end may differ. For you it can be a journey of rich awareness. For me it will be that journey transforming itself into the threshold of prayer.

My third spotlight involves the wisdom of self-change. For instance, on one important occasion I had the privilege of being a companion with you on the strange groping road to a crossroads in your life, a decision over attitudes, something born out of pain and struggle. You could have got stuck but you chose to "enlarge the size of your tent"—a great phrase from Isaiah. Perhaps each wisdom is shadowed by an opposite danger, and in this case the Enemy is clear: ruts capture us and then doors can close within us. Perhaps the first major hurdle of young adulthood is the conversion from random to reflective living, that moment when one feels called to move on from pleasant drifting and opt to focus one's freedom. You have already met that crossroads when you wanted to abandon the obvious gifts you had because they seemed burdens, obstacles to immediate experience; and it was a real wisdom that led you to choose the long-term call at the expense of short-term experience.

Later life brings different kinds of ruts and self-changes. Take the stage I'm experiencing these last years, the so-called second journey or mid-life transition. Here the landscape is different from my early twenties. It is rather the Nicodemus moment of finding it incredible that I must be born again. The demons of boredom and fatigue tempt one to give up the effort. Wisdom lies in seizing the struggle and searching yet again for painful openness.

Let me record my thanks for one particular way in which your atheism keeps my faith honest and alert. There can be a subtle danger for me of speaking about faith in too personalist a language. To speak, as even now, of the "wisdom of self-change" risks being too cosy or even narcissistic. The fire in you that makes you an active socialist is something I cherish and something I need. I need your fire to save me from too "spiritual" a reading of reality and even from too "spiritual" an interpretation of the gospels. That fire is not a matter of sporadic bouts but (as Wilfred Owen wrote from the trenches in 1917) "sympathy for the oppressed always". I see you struggling to live out that uncomfortable call and am grateful to you for it. No matter how often we say the right words, there is constantly the temptation to equate Christian faith more with some version of meaning than with some kind of lived commitment. You act as the alarm clock of my conscience there. You are my reminder that faith-doing is even more important than faith-knowing.

To return then to our topic of these pages, it would be wrong to reduce the wisdom of life's decisions to matters of the self alone. Nothing is non-political, as you like to say. Your mixture of social indignation, social compassion, and social involvement is

something Christians can be too shy of; it is something that I need
to nourish both in my thinking and in my lived choices. Your life
has specialised, so to speak, is a passion for justice; mine has been
drawn more to exploring the struggles of faith today. The two
struggles together hold the key to our world and its future. May we
long continue to cross-waken one another into a wisdom that is
costly and lived. My relationship with you brings home that is costly and lived. My relationship with you brings home to me that being
able to be an explicit Christian is rare for someone exposed to the
full blast of our complex culture. I have to live with many questions
that are not easily answered. I have to live without a harmonious
integration of my secular self and my religious self. For you faith
seems quite impossible on the level of religious beliefs or religious
belonging. But you have your own version of faith in the trust with
which you live life, and in the values that you allow to govern your
big decisions. Don't get me wrong, I am not trying to rope you into
my horizon of faith by some kind of spiritual imperialism. But I am
saying that you also have your experience of faith, and that my
religious faith is one form of the deeper human commitment that I
see myself sharing with you. Or trying to share and trying failingly
to live. You are a committed and a generous person, a truthful searcher. Perhaps that is the nearest you will be able to come to what I
call religious faith, and if so, then that is enough. The third wisdom
points to the basic options of a life as more important than the self-
interpretations. Our interpretations differ but our experiences con-
verge. Our horizons of meaning are not the same, but our striving
to live according to our lights unites us. You may find yourself continuing to reject God as an incredible concept. You may continue to
reject the Church as an incredible institution. The third wisdom is
bigger and deeper than disagreements about concepts and institutions. It unites us on the level of a decision to try to live lives of
love. It commits us to the ever-changing adventure of that option.
At the core of this third wisdom lies a courageous openness to
changing and being changed by life. And I look on this as a form of
hidden Revelation.

Now I have moved to a language where you cannot follow me,
and that I accept. But let me at least explain what I mean. Put it in a
series of *ifs:* if there is a God, and if he wants us to know him, and
if Jesus was the entry of God into humankind and history, and if

Jesus Risen continues with us through the hidden guidings of his Spirit... then there can be a hidden Revelation of God in every life where love is struggled for, and in every moment when goodness is chosen. Once more the lived realities can unite us even when the understandings divide us. My *ifs* may seem worlds away from anything that could be true for you, but I wanted to express them for you all the same in this fairly simple fashion.

Let me close with a story of another convergence between believer and atheist, a not widely known event in the life of a very well known atheist, Jean-Paul Sartre. During World War II he was imprisoned by the Nazis in a special 'stalag' for intellectuals, and he found himself the fellow-prisoner with several priests and theologians. When Christmas came round they actually persuaded him, as the only dramatist among them, to compose a Christmas play. Sartre called his play *Bariona,* and wove his plot around the gospel episode of the magi who visit the infant Jesus. Sartre played the role of Balthazar, a king who brought people to realise that there can be hope through the discovery of one's human freedom. But Sartre's play hinges on an enormous *if:* "If God had become man for me...but what God could be that crazy?"

16

EPILOGUE:
TOWARDS ANOTHER ECUMENISM

God as unbeliever!
At the opening of this book I recounted the experience of saying
Mass in a mood of atheism. It seems only right to close with an opposite experience. In fact it was another day when the Scripture at
Mass triggered off a journey of realisation. At one moment in Matthew's gospel, Jesus quotes to the Pharisees the powerful words of
Hosea in the Old Testament, the prophetic insistence that God
wants a religion of real compassion and not of ritualism: "Go and
learn the meaning of the words, *What I want is mercy, not
sacrifice*". It came home to me with searing clarity that if what I
call my faith is not the fuel of compassion, and of a compassion lived
in some concrete way, then that faith is like sacrifices without
mercy. This false faith falls short of the hopes of both God and of
humanity. From this insight, at the time of the readings, the rest of
the Mass became quietly exciting that day—in direct contrast to the
other occasion when the Liturgy of the Eucharist was painfully
hollow. Thus, the praise of God as "holy, holy, holy" was no
longer a distant reverence but a recognition of the otherness of God
beyond my smallness, and an otherness of reaching out in compassion. The words of consecration came alive as entering into the self-
giving of Jesus, his body "given up, for you". The Our Father
became larger in its "our", embracing the whole of humankind.
And the whole Mass became more what its name implies: a being
sent with God's compassion into a wounded world.

With this new awareness of an old truth, I returned to my
wonderings about unbelief today, and something fell into place.
The prophets had pictured God as angry and even bored with ritual
religion, with any cult of sacrifices that was lacking in love. Could
one not say that, faced with this kind of religion, even God
becomes an unbeliever? Because he does not believe in this reduction of his revelation into piety:

I hate your feasts. I refuse to look at your sacrifices. Let me
have no more the noise of your singing. But let justice flow
like water...This is what God asks, only this: to act justly, to
love tenderly, and to walk humbly with your God. *(Amos
5:21 ff; Micah 6:8)*.

My insight was quite simple, but a bit strange—God the unbeliever
and some of today's more searching unbelievers could share a lot of
common ground. Both react against a religion of ritual without life
and love. If so, when I come across "atheists", I have to ask to
what extent their critique of religion may not echo the unbelief of
God himself; they too could be prophets, revealing the all-too-
human reductions of faith into something less than its true self.

In this light I came again to consider the accusations of the
classical atheists of the last two hundred years, and to discover in
them a surprisingly healthy prophecy against a faith that falls short
of its fullness. For instance, one school will suspect believers of
needing a crutch to help us through life and imagining a useful God
to comfort us. Yes but. Yes: as John Calvin once put it, the human
mind is an idol-factory in constant operation, and it is indeed possible for us to retreat to a narrow religion unworthy of the real God.
But a God of mere utility is not the God of Revelation; the cosy
divinity that mankind might concoct does not square with the glory
and challenge of God in the face of Christ.

Another school will attack religion as being a drug against the
urgent transformation of this unjust world: if what matters is eter-
nity then time is hardly worth bothering about. Yes but. Yes, it can
happen that Christianity is interpreted in practice as a kind of
private property, cut off from the larger world and its crying needs.
But this divorced religion, devoid of social conscience, is another
reduction and another idolatry; and these political critiques of
religion can serve as purifications towards a fuller "praxis" of
faith.

A more psychological attack on faith might say that it is a sign
of immaturity and a product of fear. Yes but. Yes, within my living
of faith there is always ambiguity and inadequacy, and I remain
capable to a humiliating degree of regressing to infantile attitudes.
But the call of Christ is the opposite of this: to become fully alive,
to be saved from fear, and to become free to take my part of res-

ponsibility for this world. In this way, a non-aggressive and non-defensive listening to the great atheists can serve a prophetic function for believers: it can unmask the possible impoverishments of religion and remind one of the fullness of faith often unlived.

Thinking this through brought me to recognise a few paradoxes about belief and unbelief. It is all too easy for us believers to stunt our faith into something safe and uncostly and so protect ourselves from God. But this is what Jesus parodied as "Lord-Lord' religion. It is what the prophets constantly attacked. It can lurk as a subtle and even unrecognised form of unbelief within believers. And it can also be a source of unbelief for unbelievers—because they may be scandalised, and rightly, by the dishonesty of unlived faith. Thus, what sometimes passes for religion deserves the critique of atheists, just as it deserved the critique of God through the prophets. What deserves rejection is a shoddy article and not the real thing.

Pillars of a new ecumenism of believer and unbeliever
But if a listening to modern unbelief can help purify religion of some of its inadequacies in practice, the deeper encounter of believer and atheist can have a still more positive function—and this has been the experience of these last twenty years whenever the Vatican II invitation to dialogue has been taken up. Certainly my own meetings with unbelievers have cast light on my experience of faith, so that I have come to appreciate both its privilege and its fragility. From efforts at dialogue I have learned something more about the nature of faith, both in its perennial core and in its texture at the present time. Paradoxically, the encounter with atheism can cast special light on the darkness of faith, and in this respect I cherish one particular memory—not from a moment of dialogue with unbelievers, but from a meeting of priests who were considering the theme of unbelief. It was one afternoon in the south-west of Ireland, when a retired parish priest spoke in response to a presentation of mine. He spoke about having time in his retirement to read various modern theologians, and of his discovery that there were many deep and knotty problems about God and faith today, problems without easy answers. Then he added something to this effect: "Vatican I, a hundred years ago, said two important things about faith. One, that it was certain, because it depends on God,

and two, that it was also dark, because we do not have any vision of God in this life. I think we have preached to the people only one half of that twofold truth. We told them faith was certain. The time has come to share with them that it is also very dark.''

Ever since that day I have been encouraged to ponder more the non-obviousness of God, and the parallel between the experience of darkness within faith and the experience of darkness by the genuine atheist. Earlier in this book I explored the story of Thérèse of Lisieux, a mystic who found herself sharing the darkness of atheism in a strange way. In his earlier days Pope John Paul II wrote a book on the nature of faith in another mystic, St John of the Cross, and there he noted the tension between faith being both "certain and obscure". According to John of the Cross, the excessive light of God blinds the mind of man, and so the darkness we speak of stems from the human mind being incapable of being transformed into light in this life. Theologians down the ages have wondered over this theme in different ways—Paul seeing through a glass darkly, or Aquinas on faith as veiled knowledge. God always seemed silent, and distant. God was never obvious, or rather the only God who was obvious was probably not God. But in our day (as Pope Paul VI said) the Spirit speaks to the Churches through the phenomenon of atheism. If so, one of the fruits may be a new fellowship between mystic and atheist, as experiencing differently the drama of the essential darkness of faith. To acknowledge this common experience of darkness can bring believer and unbeliever to a humbling of any over-confident clarities about God or non-God. It can unite them in a relationship of new reverence before silent mystery. In this way the darkness can be at least one of the pillars of a new ecumenism between believer and unbeliever.

But there are other possible pillars which can be mentioned briefly. A few pages back I was asking whether the atheist may not sometimes be a prophet, discerning the falsity of unlived faith. Now I have been asking whether some forms of agonised and genuine atheism may not have more in common with the experiences of mystical darkness than is usually allowed for in more argumentative approaches. In this light perhaps three areas unite both believer and unbeliever today: the urge to question what is accepted, because it may be unworthy; the need to search out what is the deepest truth about humanity; and the wisdom to endure darkness on the journey. A shared critique of how things are. A shared hunger for how things might be. And a shared experience of dark unknowing before the ultimate.

What then is faith today? It is as it always was "the victory over the world" *(1 John 5:4)*. The victory can be described in many ways, but at the very least faith is a strange kind of knowing, unlike any other form of human knowledge. It is quite different from the usual journey to knowledge, starting from outer experience. Perhaps the only close parallel is the knowledge of people in love. Faith starts from being loved by God. And its strangeness was always expressed as some mixture of choosing and perceiving—in which I have to make my choice before I can perceive its truth. If faith was always the victory of a strange kind of knowing, today it will depend on our moment in history for its tonality. Today it will be more searching than sure, more personal than institutional, more complex than simple, more a victory won in the teeth of scepticism than an easy assumption of certitude. If the experience of faith today is inevitably influenced by the context of doubt all around, it will also be exposed to the more ancient conflicts of light and dark as dramatised throughout the Bible. The story there was of the ever-changing temptation to various idolatries, and even today this may well remain a deeper blockage to faith than all the pressures of modern confusions and questioning. Thus, faith today will be a victory over the world in two senses, the old meaning of the self-closed attitude and the God-proof heart, and the newer meaning of the peculiar perplexities of this world now.

But the ultimate source of faith is God and faith is knowledge born from the surprise of discovering oneself loved, if so the starting point is not manking at all, as is shown in the most revolutionary *not* in the New Testament: what is primary is *"not* our love for God but God's love for us... since God has loved us, we too should love one another". Believers have the privilege of knowing both loves, even if darkly, and of struggling to find language for both of them today. Unbelievers have the essential call of living the second love, even if the surprise of that first love remains, for many reasons, veiled from them.